Checklist for Life

Presented To:

_____

Presented By:

_____

Date:

_____

Checklist for Life

Checklist for Life

THOMAS NELSON PUBLISHERS®
Nashville

A Division of Thomas Nelson, Inc.
www.ThomasNelson.com

Scripture quotations noted NKJV are from THE NEW KING JAMES VERSION. Copyright © 1979, 1980, 1982, Thomas Nelson, Inc., Publishers.

Scripture quotations noted CEV are from THE CONTEMPORARY ENGLISH VERSION. © 1991 by the American Bible Society. Used by permission.

Scripture quotations noted GOD'S WORD are from GOD'S WORD, a copyrighted work of God's Word to the Nations Bible Society. Quotations are used by permission. Copyright 1995 by God's Word to the Nations Bible Society. All rights reserved.

Scripture quotations noted KJV are from the KING JAMES VERSION.

Scripture quotations noted THE MESSAGE are from *The Message* by Eugene H. Peterson, copyright © 1993, 1994, 1995, 1996, 2000. Used by permission of NavPress Publishing Group. All rights reserved.

Scripture quotations noted NASB are from the NEW AMERICAN STANDARD BIBLE®, © copyright The Lockman Foundation 1960, 1962, 1963, 1968, 1971, 1972, 1973, 1975, 1977, 1995. Used by permission.

Scripture quotations noted NCV are from *The Holy Bible, New Century Version*, copyright © 1987, 1988, 1991 by Word Publishing, Nashville, TN 37214. Used by permission.

Scripture quotations noted NIV are from the HOLY BIBLE: NEW INTERNATIONAL VERSION®, copyright © 1973, 1978, 1984 by International Bible Society. Used by permission of Zondervan Publishing House. All rights reserved.

Scripture quotations noted NLT are from the *Holy Bible*, New Living Translation, copyright © 1996. Used by permission of Tyndale House Publishers, Inc., Wheaton, Illinois 60189. All rights reserved.

Scripture quotations noted NRSV are from the NEW REVISED STANDARD VERSION of the Bible, copyright © 1989 by the Division of Christian Education of the National Council of The Churches of Christ in the U.S.A. All rights reserved.

Scripture quotations noted TLB are from *The Living Bible*, copyright © 1971. Used by permission of Tyndale House Publishers, Inc., Wheaton, Illinois 60189. All rights reserved.

Managing Editor: Lila Empson
Manuscript written and prepared by Steve Parolini
Design: Whisner Design Group

Checklist for life: timeless wisdom & foolproof strategies for making the most of life's challenges and opportunities.
    p. cm.
ISBN 0-7852-6455-8
1. Christian Life. I. Thomas Nelson Publishers.
BV4501.3.C46 2002
248.4—dc21
                        2002005448

Printed in the United States of America

03 04 05 06   CJK   12 11 10 09

Heart Attitude

I will be confident that God knows my heart.

Table of Contents

Table of Contents Continued

Introduction

Give me understanding, and I shall live —PSALM 119:144 NKJV

Are you prepared for life?

Life is a journey that can often lead you to unexpected places. It's an adventure with a penchant for hurling challenges and opportunities in your path. Are you equipped for the challenges? Geared up to seize the opportunities?

As any great adventurer will tell you, it's advisable to bring along the right tools when you set out on a journey. If your journey is a search for "a fulfilling and confident life," *Checklist for Life* may be just the tool set you're looking for. Whether you're in the middle of a difficult challenge today or simply preparing for the ones that will come tomorrow, this book can help you know which fork in the road you should take. When opportunities arise, it can help you make the most of your circumstances.

The sixty-six overviews or insight passages in this how-to guide explore a wide variety of topics—from fighting fear to knowing God's forgiveness to setting and reaching goals. Want to be prepared for many of life's surprises? Read the book cover to cover. Dealing with a specific challenge or opportunity? Look up the topic in the Table of Contents and study that meditation.

Immerse yourself in and anchor your life to the timeless wisdom and truth of God's Word. Explore the sensible strategies that can help you take confident steps in your life journey. Then complete the checklists. The I Will checklists guide you in reflecting on the topic and embracing the wisdom that can help you make the most of your challenge or opportunity. The Things to Do checklists provide practical ideas for applying this wisdom to your life today.

Keep Checklist for Life with you. Use it as a field guide to life's incredible journey. Feeling tired? Learn how to find rest (see "A Day for You"). Struggling with temptation? Discover how to overcome it (see "A Way Out").

Life is a big adventure. Be prepared. Bring *Checklist for Life* along for the ride.

Life is God's novel. Let him write it. —ISAAC BASHEVIS SINGER

Trust in the LORD, and do good; dwell in the land, and feed on His faithfulness.

PSALM 37:3 NKJV

Call on God, but row away from the rocks.

RALPH WALDO EMERSON

> The two most powerful warriors are patience and time.
> —LEO TOLSTOY

What is faith? It is the confident assurance that what we hope for is going to happen. It is the evidence of things we cannot yet see.

HEBREWS 11:1 THE MESSAGE

> The first duty of love is to listen.
> —PAUL TILLICH

The way from God to a human heart is through a human heart.

SAMUEL GORDON

The fruit of the Spirit is love, joy, peace, longsuffering, kindness, goodness, faithfulness, gentleness, self-control. Against such there is no law.

GALATIANS 5:22–23 NKJV

Aim at Heaven and you will get earth "thrown in": aim at earth and you will get neither.

C. S. LEWIS

Checklist for Life

Courage is almost a contradiction in terms. It means a strong desire to live taking the form of a readiness to die.
    —*G. K. Chesterton*

Let nothing be done through selfish ambition or conceit, but in lowliness of mind let each esteem others better than himself.
    —*Philippians 2:3* NKJV

Words That Matter

Jonathan, Saul's son, arose and went to David in the woods and strengthened his hand in God.

—1 SAMUEL 23:16 NKJV

Take a moment to think about someone who is a close friend. Can you recall a time when that person was merely an acquaintance? What was it that took your relationship from acquaintance to friend? A shared interest? Passion for a common cause? Perhaps a heated debate? However your friendship began, things are probably quite different in your relationship today. The polite "hello" of acquaintance days has grown into a vocabulary of deeper relationship, which includes spoken as well as unspoken sentiments.

Jonathan was just such a friend to David. David was hiding in the wilderness, attempting to discern God's will while simultaneously avoiding detection by Saul, who sought his life. Jonathan, Saul's son, came to David with words of encouragement, saying, "Do not fear, for the hand of Saul my father shall not find you. You shall be king over Israel, and I shall be next to you" (1 Samuel 23:17). These words from a mere acquaintance might have been received with a smile and a thank-you, or maybe one of those you-don't-know-what-you're-talking-about looks. Yet those were words of encouragement from a true friend, and so the words mattered. Jonathan's words could be trusted.

The trusted words of a friend can make a positive impact in your life. Listening requires humility, patience, and an open mind.

Start with humility—know that you aren't always right. It's okay to admit you're not perfect when you're with a trusted friend. Remember, your friend is on your side.

Next, be patient. Let the wise counsel seep into you and steep there for a while. Don't jump to a wrong conclusion or criticize your friend's words before you've really examined them. It may be tough to hear some of your friend's words, but you'll never get the chance if you're calculating your response while your friend is still speaking.

Finally, be prepared to have your best-laid plans turned upside down, or at least sideways. Sometimes a friend will propose a solution you hadn't even considered—one that doesn't make sense at first. An open mind allows you to approach new ideas willingly.

Take the encouragement of a friend to heart. Let the words strengthen you. Even if you fail or fall, those words will provide a softer landing place. That's because the encouraging words of a true friend are inseparable from the unspoken message of friendship—a message of love.

I Will

Listen for God's direction in the encouraging words of a friend.

yes _____ _no_ _____

Trust that God can use my friends to help me grow.

yes _____ _no_ _____

Understand that a good friend is a gift from God.

yes _____ _no_ _____

Listen to a friend's words as intently as I would want my friend to listen to me.

yes _____ _no_ _____

Know that a friend's words are usually spoken out of concern.

yes _____ _no_ _____

Learn to embrace a friend's words.

yes _____ _no_ _____

Attempt to encourage my friends as often as possible.

yes _____ _no_ _____

Things to Do

☐ _Pray for wisdom to know how to encourage others._

☐ _Write a thank-you note today to one friend who has encouraged you._

☐ _Be prepared to offer a few words of encouragement to a friend._

☐ _Invite a friend to consult with you on an upcoming decision._

☐ _Call a friend to say how much you appreciate his or her friendship._

☐ _Read about David and Jonathan's friendship in 1 Samuel, chapters 19 and 20._

☐ _Offer your friendship to someone with whom you'd like to have a closer relationship._

Things to Remember

A friend loves at all times, and a brother is born for adversity.

PROVERBS 17:17 NKJV

Greater love has no one than this, than to lay down one's life for his friends.

JOHN 15:13 NKJV

A man who has friends must himself be friendly, but there is a friend who sticks closer than a brother.

PROVERBS 18:24 NKJV

Wounds from a friend can be trusted, but an enemy multiplies kisses.

PROVERBS 27:6 NIV

No longer do I call you servants, for a servant does not know what his master is doing; but I have called you friends, for all things that I heard from My Father I have made known to you.

JOHN 15:15 NKJV

Encourage each other every day while it is "today." Help each other so none of you will become hardened because sin has tricked you.

HEBREWS 3:13 NCV

It is mutual respect which makes friendship lasting.

—JOHN HENRY NEWMAN

God evidently does not intend us all to be rich or powerful or great, but He does intend us all to be friends.

—RALPH WALDO EMERSON

Patience

Hurry Up and Wait

*I, therefore, the prisoner of the Lord, beseech you to walk
worthy of the calling with which you were called, with all
lowliness and gentleness, with longsuffering, bearing with one
another in love.*

—EPHESIANS 4:1–2 NKJV

Patience is a desirable trait—one that paints a picture of
peace in the midst of chaos. It is a bit ironic that people who
cry out for it do so with the subtlety of a charging rhino.

Perhaps you've spoken these words aloud (or under your
breath) once or twice. If so, you're in good company. Parents,
children, teenagers, grandparents, office-workers, bosses,
pastors, and pew-sitters have all uttered these words. In fact,
probably anyone who's ever spent more than a few minutes
with another person has had ample opportunity to consider
the necessity of patience. Wherever two or more are gathered
together, patience is required.

The apostle Paul spoke often about being patient. He
encouraged new Christians to "bear with one another in love."
He knew that the excitement of this new thing called
Christianity would have all sorts of ramifications in people's
daily lives. This would invariably lead to disputes and

disagreements, all in the effort to do the right thing. He knew that a group of five people might have ten opinions on the same topic. And he knew that, without patience, those people might turn against each other before discovering their common ground or learning to compromise. (Sound familiar?)

Do you find that you spend much of your life trying to maintain a rhythm that blends into the many different paths that other people walk? That rhythm is often changeable, and it is often disrupted. Trying to fit with it often appears to be nearly impossible. And you know you need patience. That leads to the first step: Accept that the world doesn't always dance in time with you. Simply acknowledging the fact that few things will ever work according to your timetable. That acknowledgment is a huge step toward embracing patience.

Here's another: Slow down before responding. Take time to think things through. Stay focused on the topic and give yourself times to reflect. In a fast-food world, try not to respond with a fast-food philosophy.

Seek first to understand, not to be understood. Take time to examine the situation. Do you have all the details right? Maybe your impatience is warranted, or maybe it is based on misinformation.

Be deliberate about talking to God. Set aside time each day to ask Him for a greater storehouse of patience. Ask for wisdom to know how to respond with patience in patience-trying situations.

Finally, know that growing patience takes time. You may not get it "right now," but if you truly desire patience, you will find it.

I Will

Pray for wisdom to know when I should practice patience.

<u>yes</u>   <u>no</u>

Ask God for patience when I know it's needed in a given situation.

<u>yes</u>   <u>no</u>

Expect to find myself in situations where patience is required.

<u>yes</u>   <u>no</u>

Know that everyone faces the challenge of learning to be patient.

<u>yes</u>   <u>no</u>

Learn from past experience how impatience leads to division.

<u>yes</u>   <u>no</u>

Look at Paul's example to learn how to develop patience.

<u>yes</u>   <u>no</u>

Things to Do

☐ *Review a recent experience that challenged your patience and examine what made being patient so difficult.*

☐ *Identify a coworker, family member, or friend and observe how this person handles patience.*

☐ *Participate in an activity once (such as playing a board game with friends) that gives you a chance to practice patience.*

☐ *List three everyday opportunities you have to practice patience (while shopping, working, sharing a meal with friends).*

☐ *Write a letter to God asking for more patience.*

☐ *Talk with a friend you respect about how he or she practices patience.*

Things to Remember

The end of a thing is better than its beginning; the patient in spirit is better than the proud in spirit.

ECCLESIASTES 7:8 NKJV

A hot-tempered man stirs up dissension, but a patient man calms a quarrel.

PROVERBS 15:18 NIV

We show we are servants of God by our pure lives, our understanding, patience, and kindness, by the Holy Spirit, by true love.

2 CORINTHIANS 6:6 NCV

The Lord is not slack concerning His promise, as some count slackness, but is longsuffering toward us, not willing that any should perish but that all should come to repentance.

2 PETER 3:9 NKJV

For many years You had patience with them, and testified against them by Your Spirit in Your prophets. Yet they would not listen; therefore You gave them into the hand of the peoples of the lands.

NEHEMIAH 9:30 NKJV

Rest in the Lord, and wait patiently for Him.

PSALM 37:7 NKJV

Patience means living out the belief that God orders everything for the spiritual good of his children.

—J. I. PACKER

The two most powerful warriors are patience and time.

—LEO TOLSTOY

Hope

The Now and the Not-Yet

Blessed be the God and Father of our Lord Jesus Christ, who according to His abundant mercy has begotten us again to a living hope through the resurrection of Jesus Christ from the dead.

—*1 Peter 1:3 NKJV*

Real hope is one of the most reached-for brass rings in today's wildly spinning world. Though many people may not truly know what it is they're reaching for, they instinctively know it's something big.

They're right. Far greater than the more common desires for wealth, status, health, or power, real hope is a longing for significance, an ache for meaning. You may have first caught a glimpse of this hope when life was particularly difficult. Or it may have sneaked up on you when things were going along just fine.

This hope for a meaningful life is the very hope that Jesus promises to fulfill for those who choose to follow Him. It is fulfilled with a twofold pledge: the promise for a full and significant life today and the guarantee of paradise tomorrow. It is the promise of the now and the not-yet.

The not-yet aspect of this hope is the easiest to grasp. This is the promise of heaven for all who follow Jesus. What a hope that is—no more pain or suffering coupled with life everlasting that is infinitely richer than your best day on earth. A picture of heaven is pretty easy to paint—especially during a time when the world around you looks pretty bleak.

But that's a hope for tomorrow. The now aspect of Jesus' hope can fuel every today with promise. It is the confident assurance that God is on your side. If you don't get a desired promotion, it is the assurance that God values you just as much as if you had won the new job. If a storm ruins your family vacation, it is the confidence that—unlike the weather—God will never change. If reconciliation fails because of a few poorly chosen words, it is the knowledge that God will love you no matter what you say to Him.

The first step to receiving these benefits of real hope is straightforward: Choose to follow Christ and the now and not-yet are yours. Hanging on to these benefits in everyday life isn't always so easy. That's because you experience pain, disappointment, and trials. In these times, hope, though desired, is often a slippery thing to grasp.

One way to hang on to hope is to look ahead to the promise of heaven. Even in the most challenging life situation, a glimpse into the future can keep you moving forward. Knowing that God's promise of a life without pain is coming "some day" may be just enough to get you through the pain of today.

You can also find hope by recalling those past moments when hope shone through a dark time. You've held on to hope before . . . you know what it tastes like. Revisit those times when you need a new infusion of hope. Sometimes just remembering the way hope surprised you can bring you a new portion of hope for the current situation.

Another way to discover hope is to look around and see where God is in the middle of your difficult time. One of the greatest promises in the Bible is that God will always be there. Sometimes He is there to take away the pain. Sometimes He is there to comfort you in the midst of pain. And other times, often to your dismay, He is there to teach you something significant through the trials. But no matter the circumstance, God is there.

There will be times when you feel that hope has deserted you. God has provided ways for you to find hope again. If you can't see Him, pray. Ask God to reveal the hope that will get you through your challenging times. Call a trusted friend and ask for encouraging words. Seek God's promises in the Bible. The book of Psalms is packed with both the promise of hope and the aching desire to regain it. The now hope is always available, but sometimes it takes a little exploration to find it.

Go ahead and hope. Know that God is with you when your hopes are fulfilled and when they vanish. Trust the Living Hope. And look forward to the promise of heaven. If you know Jesus, you're going to see just how fantastic it is.

My people will be happy forever
because of the things I will make.
I will make a Jerusalem that is full of joy,
and I will make her people a delight.
—ISAIAH 65:18 NCV

I Will

Examine what it means to hope in God.   _yes_   _no_

Ask God to send a reminder of hope when life gets
tough.   _yes_   _no_

Learn to embrace the now aspect of Jesus' hope.   _yes_   _no_

Look forward to the hope of heaven.   _yes_   _no_

Know that some things I hope for will occur while
others won't.   _yes_   _no_

Continue to hope for good things.   _yes_   _no_

Things to Do

☐ Look up hope in a traditional dictionary and then again in a Bible
dictionary. Compare the definitions.

☐ Study Bible passages that tell about heaven and then draw your own
picture of what heaven might be like.

☐ Make a list of hopes and dreams you have.

☐ Create a hope-reminder card to keep in your purse or wallet and refer
to it often (consider copying 1 Peter 1:3 on it).

☐ Talk with a friend about how he or she deals with times when hope
seems distant.

☐ Watch a movie that tackles the topic of hope and compare the movie's
approach to the hope God promises to those who follow Him.

Things to Remember

Why are you cast down, O my soul? and why are you disquieted within me? Hope in God, for I shall yet praise Him for the help of His countenance.

Psalm 42:5 NKJV

The people who trust the LORD will become strong again. They will rise up as an eagle in the sky; they will run and not need rest; they will walk and not become tired.

Isaiah 40:31 NCV

> *Those who fear You will be glad when they see me, because I have hoped in Your word.*
> —Psalm 119:74 NKJV

We were saved in this hope, but hope that is seen is not hope; for why does one still hope for what he sees?

Romans 8:24 NKJV

"I know the plans I have for you," declares the LORD, "plans to prosper you and not to harm you, plans to give you hope and a future."

Jeremiah 29:11 NIV

[God's grace] teaches us not to live against God nor to do the evil things the world wants to do. Instead, that grace teaches us to live now in a wise and right way and in a way that shows we serve God. We should live like that while we wait for our great hope and the coming of the glory of our great God and Savior Jesus Christ.

TITUS 2:12–13 NCV

To this end we both labor and suffer reproach, because we trust in the living God, who is the Savior of all men, especially of those who believe.

1 TIMOTHY 4:10 NKJV

If we hope for what we do not yet have, we wait for it patiently.

ROMANS 8:25 NIV

O Israel, hope in the LORD; for with the LORD there is mercy, and with Him is abundant redemption.

PSALM 130:7 NKJV

God decided to let his people know this rich and glorious secret which he has for all people. This secret Is Christ himself, who is in you. He is our only hope for glory.

COLOSSIANS 1:27 NCV

Hope is never ill when faith is well.

—JOHN BUNYAN

No man is able of himself to grasp the supreme good of eternal life; he needs divine help. Hence there is here a two-fold object, the eternal life we hoped for, and the divine help we hope by.

—SAINT THOMAS AQUINAS

Dealing with Anger

Counting to Ten

"Be angry, and do not sin": Do not let the sun go down on your wrath.

—*Ephesians 4:26* NKJV

Have you ever felt angry toward a person or situation and wondered if your feelings were appropriate? Has your anger ever caused you to say or do something you later regretted? You're not alone. Anger is a universally expressed human emotion. It also happens to sit near the top of the least-comfortable-feelings list.

You have heard it said that when you're nearing the boiling point you should count to ten. Only one small problem: In the middle of your frustration, you probably prefer to count backward. "Ten . . . nine . . . eight . . . seven . . . six . . . five . . . four . . . three . . . two . . . one . . . *boom!* Angry countdowns rarely end with a calm, relaxed resolution. They usually end in disaster.

Or maybe instead of overreacting in anger, you try to ignore your very real feelings. Perhaps you bottle up anger and hope it goes away. But it doesn't go away; it hangs around. Bottled-up anger actually stays "fresh" longer.

What can you do? How should you respond when

someone or something triggers your anger switch? First, take time to examine the situation before responding. Is this something that warrants a response? What kind of response? Are you simply frustrated, or does your anger stem from a desire to right a wrong? A quick temper tries to make things right too soon and may escalate rather than solve the situation. If you have a tendency to react in anger, pray for patience. Allow yourself time to understand.

Then carefully consider your next step. Perhaps you can work things out through a calm discussion. Maybe you need to step away from the situation—create some space so you don't respond inappropriately. Or maybe you should invite a third party to help bring a new perspective to the situation.

You'll need good judgment in order to resolve your anger. And resolution is the key to dealing with anger appropriately. Paul emphasized this when he wrote: "Do not let the sun go down while you are still angry." You probably know from experience how damaging unresolved anger can be. Don't get stuck there. If you are attempting to right a wrong, bathe your attitude and thoughts in love before confronting the object of your anger—and then do so as soon as possible.

Your final step is to look inward. Maybe there's a lesson in this for you. Do you need to build perseverance? grow tolerance? develop a gentle spirit? God has filled your life with opportunities to grow—both in your understanding of the human condition, and in your relationship with Him. Seek God's truth in the middle of your anger, and growth will be assured.

I Will

Seek God's wisdom when faced with a situation that has prompted my anger. _____ yes _____ no

Make sure I'm not letting anger control me before I confront a situation. _____ yes _____ no

Acknowledge that sometimes it's okay to be angry. _____ yes _____ no

Attempt to understand what might have prompted the object of my anger to act in the way he or she did. _____ yes _____ no

Take time to understand what triggers my anger in a given situation. _____ yes _____ no

Look for a life lesson from God when evaluating my anger. _____ yes _____ no

Things to Do

☐ *List things that anger you the most.*

☐ *Pray for wisdom to avoid inappropriate anger.*

☐ *Attempt reconciliation for an unresolved situation in which you responded with anger.*

☐ *Make a sign that says* COUNT TO TEN *(or some other reminder not to overreact) and place it in a visible location in your home.*

☐ *Read a book or article on dealing with anger.*

☐ *Ask a friend to hold you accountable to your desire to seek understanding instead of retaliation.*

☐ *Make a list of situations where your anger may be appropriate.*

Things to Remember

The discerning heart seeks knowledge, but the mouth of a fool feeds on folly.

PROVERBS 15:14 NIV

The discretion of a man makes him slow to anger, and his glory is to overlook a transgression.

PROVERBS 19:11 NKJV

Do not hasten in your spirit to be angry, for anger rests in the bosom of fools.

ECCLESIASTES 7:9 NKJV

You are a forgiving God. You are kind and full of mercy. You do not become angry quickly, and you have great love. So you did not leave them.

NEHEMIAH 9:17 NCV

Let every man be swift to hear, slow to speak, slow to wrath.

JAMES 1:19 NKJV

He who is slow to wrath has great understanding, but he who is impulsive exalts folly.

PROVERBS 14:29 NKJV

Don't sin by letting anger gain control over you.

PSALM 4:4 NLT

How much more grievous are the consequences of anger than the causes of it.
—MARCUS AURELIUS

Never ascribe to an opponent motives meaner than your own.
—JOHN M. BARRIE

Helping Others

Act Backward

Jesus said, "If I then, your Lord and Teacher, have washed your feet, you also ought to wash one another's feet."

—*John 13:14* NKJV

For many people, life is a series of actions with the same focused intent: taking care of number one. These are the people who shout with both words and deeds, "It's all about me!" You may know one or two at the office, school, or even at home.

It's no surprise that a lifestyle promoting selfish service is so prevalent today. A barrage of popular media is constantly telling you that the only person who's really important in this world is you. But the it's-all-about-me philosophy isn't a recent phenomenon. It's been around for ages.

That's probably why the self-important religious leaders in Jesus' time were so taken aback when Jesus spoke about serving others. "Whoever desires to be great among you, let him be your servant," He said. *What? That's backward!* they must have thought.

Jesus didn't stop at words, though. He took on one of the lowliest tasks—foot washing—to show His disciples just how to be a servant. This wasn't a grandstanding or look-at-me event. (Sandals and dusty roads made for particularly dirty feet.) It was a humble, quiet action that taught a simple yet powerful lesson: serve others unselfishly.

Jesus reinforced this lesson by asking that the disciples do as he had done. That's the challenge you face today. Do you help others unselfishly? Or are your wants stacked up so high you can't even see your own feet, let alone your neighbors'?

Serving others requires sacrifice. If you volunteer to help a neighbor with a project, you may miss your favorite television show. But that's okay. Consider what you're really missing by giving something up to help another person. Is this thing really all that important to you? Is it necessary? If the answer is yes, then stay with your original plan. But if the answer is an honest, no, consider giving it up. Your sacrifice, no matter how small, will turn into gold when you help someone else with a need.

Serving others might also mean risking the ridicule or disdain of those who believe only in serving themselves. The risk is worth it. Most people who observe your unselfish act will be inspired. Stay focused on the task at hand—helping someone—and perhaps you'll even inspire others to also reconsider and appreciate the value of serving others.

Reaching out to others instead of always taking care of number one is worth the sacrifice. You are never as tall in God's sight as when you are on your knees, washing someone's feet. Make helping others a new priority in your life.

I Will

Learn from Jesus' example how to serve others
without fear of what others will think of me.

_____ *yes* _____ *no*

Ask God to teach me how to be unselfish in a world
that preaches a self-serving lifestyle.

_____ *yes* _____ *no*

Know that God is pleased when I help others.

_____ *yes* _____ *no*

Look for opportunities to serve.

_____ *yes* _____ *no*

Seek to understand what it means to serve
unselfishly.

_____ *yes* _____ *no*

Examine my heart to see if I am being too selfish.

_____ *yes* _____ *no*

Things to Do

☐ *Pray for God to reduce your wants and increase your willingness to serve.*

☐ *Study what the Bible teaches about serving others (begin with the Scriptures listed on the facing page).*

☐ *Do something unexpected to help a friend—but don't seek acknowledgment for your action.*

☐ *Examine what you own and determine how you might use it to serve others.*

☐ *Volunteer to cook a meal for a neighbor or friend.*

☐ *Come up with three ways you can help a family member in the coming week and implement them.*

Things to Remember

You, brethren, have been called to liberty; only do not use liberty as an opportunity for the flesh, but through love serve one another.

GALATIANS 5:13 NKJV

Don't just do what you have to do to get by, but work heartily, as Christ's servants doing what God wants you to do.

EPHESIANS 6:6 THE MESSAGE

Whoever desires to become great among you, let him be your servant. And whoever desires to be first among you, let him be your slave—just as the Son of Man did not come to be served, but to serve, and to give His life a ransom for many.

MATTHEW 20:26–28 NKJV

What, after all, is Apollos? And what is Paul? Only servants, through whom you came to believe—as the Lord has assigned to each his task.

1 CORINTHIANS 3:5 NIV

Seek the LORD, all you meek of the earth, who have upheld His justice. Seek righteousness, seek humility.

ZEPHANIAH 2:3 NKJV

The service we render for others is really the rent we pay for our room on this earth.

—WILFRED GRENFELL

The service that counts is the service that costs.

—HOWARD HENDRICKS

Still, Small Voice

To the pure all things are pure, but to those who are defiled and unbelieving nothing is pure; but even their mind and conscience are defiled.

—Titus 1:15 NKJV

Have you ever stopped in the middle of an activity because an internal voice was warning you of potentially negative consequences? Or paused mid-sentence because that same voice was cautioning you that your words might be unnecessarily hurtful? That little voice is what some might call your conscience. But what is your conscience? And is it trustworthy?

If cartoons are to be believed, your conscience wears angel wings and sits on one of your shoulders, offering the good-guy advice that is in sharp contrast to the devilish suggestions from the character with the pointy tail on your other shoulder. Amazingly, dictionaries seem to agree. The *American Heritage Dictionary* defines conscience as "the awareness of a moral or ethical aspect to one's conduct together with the urge to prefer right over wrong." Just like that little angel. The *Random House Webster's Unabridged Dictionary* says it this way: "the inner sense of what is right or wrong in one's conduct or motives, impelling one toward right action." And *Merriam-Webster's Collegiate Dictionary* says: "the sense of the consciousness of the moral goodness or blameworthiness of one's own conduct, intentions, or character together with a feeling of obligation to do right or be good."

But there's a problem. Who's to say what's "right" and what's "wrong"? What source does this little voice reference to determine that which is considered moral or ethical? Good question. In his letter to Titus, Paul suggested that a conscience can be bad as well as good. He also pointed out the difference between the two.

Without the anchor of a relationship with God, a conscience is nothing more than a reasonable facsimile of morality—something pieced together out of societal norms and worldly wisdom. For those who know God, however, that which they call conscience is most likely guidance from the creator of morality: God in His Spirit. Working from the inside out, God's Spirit can nudge you toward intelligent decisions on what to say and what to do—and what not to say or what not to do.

Does that mean everything you hear from the voice in your head is a directive from God? Probably not. But if you desire to know God and to do His will, more often than not the voice you hear whispering advice will be the still small voice of God. It's a voice worth listening to.

I Will

Ask God to allow His Spirit to guide my
decisions.

yes _____ no _____

Look for ways to grow my understanding of how
God's Spirit works in my life.

yes _____ no _____

Trust God to send His wisdom when I face challenges
or uncertain circumstances.

yes _____ no _____

Evaluate how well I've listened to the still small
voice of God.

yes _____ no _____

Examine past decisions when I've listened to my
conscience and when I've ignored it.

yes _____ no _____

Take time to consider important decisions so I can
be sure not to miss God's guidance.

yes _____ no _____

Things to Do

☐ *Examine what the Bible has to say about the conscience.*

☐ *Pray that God would make clear the right thing to do in every situation you face.*

☐ *Talk with a friend about the role of the conscience in everyday decisions.*

☐ *Keep track of times you listen to your conscience and times you ignore your conscience. Compare the results of your decisions.*

☐ *Ask your pastor how the Holy Spirit works as your conscience.*

☐ *Invite a trusted friend to help you sort out the guidance of the Holy Spirit from other direction offered by your conscience.*

Things to Remember

Our conscience testifies that we have conducted ourselves in the world, and especially in our relations with you, in the holiness and sincerity that are from God. We have done so not according to worldly wisdom but according to God's grace.

2 CORINTHIANS 1:12 NIV

Pray for us; for we are confident that we have a good conscience, in all things desiring to live honorably.

HEBREWS 13:18 NKJV

Let us draw near with a true heart in full assurance of faith, having our hearts sprinkled from an evil conscience and our bodies washed with pure water.

HEBREWS 10:22 NKJV

We have renounced the hidden things of shame, not walking in craftiness nor handling the word of God deceitfully, but by manifestation of the truth commending ourselves to every man's conscience in the sight of God.

2 CORINTHIANS 4:2 NKJV

I am in Christ, and I am telling you the truth; I do not lie. My conscience is ruled by the Holy Spirit, and it tells me I am not lying.

ROMANS 9:1 NCV

My conscience is captive to the Word of God. I will not recant anything, for to go against conscience is neither honest nor safe.

—MARTIN LUTHER

"Let your conscience be your guide" is only valid if God's Word is guiding your conscience.

—ANONYMOUS

Praise

Beyond Words

All together now—applause for God! Sing songs to the tune of his glory, set glory to the rhythms of his praise.

—Psalm 66:1 THE MESSAGE

You hear it at concerts, sports events, and pep rallies. It erupts after children's plays, powerful speeches, and particularly excellent movies. A crowd of thousands or an audience of one can offer it. Sometimes shouts and cheers accompany it. Other times it alone breaks the silence. It is applause.

Everyone loves applause. People long for the confirmation that they performed above expectations. They long to be praised for a job well done. You see, that's what prompts applause: a job well done. And when that applause is just for you, you soak it up like a thirsty sponge. You hang on to it fiercely—you don't want the feeling of appreciation to go away.

God wants applause too. But the applause God desires is different from the applause you might seek. God wants applause for who He is, and not just for what He has done. He wants to be praised.

It's pretty easy to say "Nice work, God!" when you're sitting on a blanket watching a warm breeze blow over a field of sunflowers yielding in a lake of yellow and brown. It's no big stretch to give God a virtual high-five when someone you care about chooses to change course and follow Christ.

Praise is a way of recognizing God for who He is and of acknowledging His glory. It's a way of saying, "You are so much bigger than my mind and heart can possibly grasp—yet I long to tell You how much I love You anyway."

Songwriters seem to understand praise better than anyone. David and other psalmists sure knew how to acknowledge God's glory. "Praise the LORD! Praise Him in the heights! Praise Him, all His angels; Praise Him, all His hosts! Praise Him, sun and moon; Praise Him, all you stars of light!" wrote one psalmist (Psalm 148:1–3 NKJV). Songwriter Rich Mullins got it, too, when he wrote "Our God is an awesome God."

Singing a hymn or other song that speaks of God's magnificence is a great way to praise Him. You'll find that most churches today take time for praise and worship in their weekly services. Go ahead and sing. Your local bookstore is also well stocked with praise and worship CDs. Put one on the CD player and let it lead you closer to God.

But there are other ways to praise God. You can praise God in your prayers. It's important to note that praise looks a little different from other kinds of prayer. You probably already thank God for all the things He does for you. If you want to praise God, thank Him also for who He is. Thank Him for His power. Thank Him that He is loving and just. By recognizing God's characteristics in your prayers, you are praising Him.

You can praise God by serving Him. When you give sacrificially to make a difference in the lives of others, you are also worshiping God. Your willingness to be used by God is acknowledgment of God's power and love.

Another way to praise God is to enjoy something that points you to the bigness of God. God's fingerprints can be found all across Creation. In those transcendent moments when a sunset or a baby's first cry lead you to be thankful, you are praising the uniqueness of the Creator. Go on a nature walk and embrace God's creativity. Go to a playground and swing on a swing to experience a taste of the freedom and joy that permeate God's nature. Hug a family member or friend and take pleasure in the fact that you both were created in God's image.

The book of Psalms is packed with examples of praise. If you're unsure what to say, look for a psalm that shouts of God's majesty. Embrace the words as your own.

Praise God in any way you can think of. Don't let the seeming insignificance of your words or actions stop you from praising. Tell God how much you wish you had the words that could describe your love for Him. Sit in silence. Bask in the indescribable wonder of God's greatness. Smile. Cheer. Applaud. God desires and deserves your praise.

As He was now drawing near the descent of the Mount of Olives, the whole multitude of the disciples began to rejoice and praise God with a loud voice for all the mighty works they had seen.
—LUKE 19:37 NKJV

I Will

Seek opportunities to praise God in everyday situations.

yes _____ no _____

Learn how to praise God for who He is and not just what He has done in my life.

yes _____ no _____

Know that God wants to be praised.

yes _____ no _____

Enjoy the unique opportunity to applaud the Creator of the universe.

yes _____ no _____

Look for new ways to praise God.

yes _____ no _____

Be confident that God knows my heart when I attempt to praise Him.

yes _____ no _____

Things to Do

☐ *Write out your praises to God each day for a week.*

☐ *Ask friends to share how they praise God. Consider trying one of their ideas.*

☐ *Sing along with a favorite praise CD.*

☐ *Paint or draw a picture depicting how you feel about God's greatness.*

☐ *Spend a half-hour in silence, reflecting only on the majesty of God.*

☐ *Read Psalms 9, 33, and 150. Then write your own.*

☐ *Visit two new-to-you church worship services to experience how other people praise God.*

Things to Remember

O LORD, I will praise you with all my heart, and tell everyone about the marvelous things you do.

PSALM 9:1 TLB

The LORD is my strength and song, and He has become my salvation; He is my God, and I will praise Him; my father's God, and I will exalt Him.

EXODUS 15:2 NKJV

I proclaim the name of the LORD: Ascribe greatness to our God.
—Deuteronomy 32:3 NKJV

Sing to Him, sing psalms to Him; talk of all His wondrous works!

PSALM 105:2 NKJV

I will praise the Lord no matter what happens. I will constantly speak of his glories and grace.

PSALM 34:1 TLB

Is any among you suffering? Let him pray. Is anyone cheerful? Let him sing psalms.

JAMES 5:13 NKJV

David praised the LORD in the presence of the whole assembly: "O LORD, the God of our ancestor Israel, may you be praised forever and ever!"

1 CHRONICLES 29:10 NLT

All the angels were standing around the throne and around the elders and the four living beings. And they fell face down before the throne and worshiped God.

REVELATION 7:11 NLT

Daniel answered and said: "Blessed be the name of God forever and ever, for wisdom and might are His."

DANIEL 2:20 NKJV

I will praise the LORD, and everyone on earth will bless his holy name forever and forever.

PSALM 145:21 NLT

Jesus said, "Nevertheless do not rejoice in this, that the spirits are subject to you, but rejoice that your names are recorded in heaven."

LUKE 10:20 NASB

Yes, the LORD has done amazing things for us! What joy!

PSALM 126:3 NLT

Wash your face every morning in a bath of praise.

—CHARLES SPURGEON

The most acceptable service we can do and show unto God, and which alone he desires of us, is that he be praised of us.

—MARTIN LUTHER

Anxiety

Look at the Birds

Jesus said to His disciples, "Therefore I say to you, do not worry about your life, what you will eat; nor about the body, what you will put on."
—Luke 12:22 NKJV

Life is packed with opportunities for anxiety. Just seeing the word worry in print can quicken your pulse. In the extreme, worry can immobilize you. It can encroach on your freedom. It can cause physical as well as psychological damage.

Not all worrying is bad, however. In fact, anxiety can have a purpose. It can raise your sensitivity to potential threats. It can prepare you for the possibility of pain. And it can underline your concern for another person.

Jesus' disciples had plenty to be worried about. To begin with, they had given up their livelihood to follow Jesus. They traded security for an unknown future. They exchanged the comfort of home for unending travel to uncertain destinations. And even though they were undeniably compelled to follow Jesus, they must have still maintained doubts about who He really was. Talk about anxiety!

Jesus knew of their worries. Yet instead of simply

brushing their concerns aside with a casual don't-worry-be-happy message, he turned their worry toward an insight into the God they desired to know better. "God will take care of the basics," he told them. "Look at the birds . . . doesn't God feed them?" Jesus taught His disciples not only about God's provision, but also about the need to refocus their priorities, about the need to have more faith, and about the relative impotence of worrying.

One of the easiest ways to reduce your anxiety is to identify those things you have no power to change. If what you're anxious about is completely out of your control, the worry is essentially useless. Acknowledge the fact that you can't change the situation and move on.

Another way to reduce your anxiety is to reprioritize your life. Do you have too many responsibilities or expectations vying for your attention? Maybe you need to devote less time to extracurricular activities and take more time for yourself. Perhaps you should take on fewer projects at work. Look for ways to remove things from your list. Determine which activities you absolutely must do and shrink the list of those that are optional.

Ask for help. Tell someone about your anxiety. A trusted friend can help you determine which worries are warranted, and which are hampering your ability to perform. Seek wise advice and listen to it. And don't be afraid to enjoy life.

Don't let your worries grow bigger than your faith in a God who can help you through the anxiety. Too much worrying eats away at your ability to live life to its fullest. Get rid of excess worries. Trade them for more trust in God.

I Will

Hand off my anxiety to God and learn to trust Him
with my worries.   yes   no

Be thankful that God cares enough for me to take
care of the "basics" of life.   yes   no

Know that not all worrying is bad.   yes   no

Consider the anxiety the disciples must have
experienced in comparison to my own list of worries.   yes   no

Examine how I can grow more faith in God so my
worry list can shrink.   yes   no

Know that it is okay to ask for help.   yes   no

Things to Do

☐ Ask God for a greater faith that can reduce your anxiety.

☐ Look up the word anxiety in a concordance and read the associated
   Bible verses.

☐ Go to a park and watch the birds for an hour. Then thank God that He
   cares for you even more than He does the birds.

☐ Make a list of the things you worry about and determine which might
   be unnecessary worries.

☐ List three things you can stop worrying about.

☐ Recall the last time you experienced a lot of anxiety. How did your
   worries play out in the resolution of the situation?

☐ Talk with a friend about how he or she deals with worry.

Things to Remember

Cast all your anxiety on him, because he cares for you.

1 PETER 5:7 NRSV

Be anxious for nothing, but in everything by prayer and supplication, with thanksgiving, let your requests be made known to God.

PHILIPPIANS 4:6 NKJV

Jesus said, "Don't worry about the food or drink you need to live, or about the clothes you need for your body. Life is more than food, and the body is more than clothes."

MATTHEW 6:25 NCV

Trust in the LORD, and do good; dwell in the land, and feed on His faithfulness.

PSALM 37:3 NKJV

Which of you by worrying can add one cubit to his stature?

MATTHEW 6:27 NKJV

All mankind scratches for its daily bread, but your heavenly Father knows your needs.

LUKE 12:30 TLB

Worry is putting question marks where God has put periods.

—JOHN R. RICE

Worry is the interest we pay on tomorrow's troubles.

—E. STANLEY JONES

Prayer

The Closet Door

Jesus said, "When you pray, you shall not be like the hypocrites. For they love to pray standing in the synagogues and on the corners of the streets, that they may be seen by men. Assuredly, I say to you, they have their reward."

—*Matthew 6:5 NKJV*

In almost every area of life, there is a persistent pressure to perform. Except, perhaps, in prayer. There are no rules for prayer. And there is no cosmic scorecard, though you wouldn't know it from the way some of the Pharisees in Jesus' day prayed.

The Pharisees prayed loudly, publicly, and with the seeming intent of drawing attention to themselves. Prayer was an event to behold. It was a chance to impress. Jesus wasn't impressed. He directly challenged the Pharisees' grandstanding by saying, "Don't be like the hypocrites when you pray." Jesus was saying that prayer is not a competition. Prayers aren't recorded in a heavenly performance evaluation and saved for a posthumous review.

Prayer is simply this: communicating with God. It is expressing your thoughts, feelings, concerns, fears, desires, hopes, and praise to God, who also happens to be the Creator of the universe.

Prayer can also be an instinctive, heart feeling. It can be an unspoken yearning, a thankfulness, a gratitude, an attitude.

The idea that you can talk directly with the Creator of the universe might seem a bit imposing at first. What could you possibly say that would be important enough for God to want to listen? Hearing talented pastors or other leaders pray with intricately crafted, ornately decorated words often compounds this trepidation. How could your prayers possibly compare to those works of art?

They don't have to. Go ahead and enjoy the beautiful prayers of others, but know that God isn't looking for great oratory from you. He's looking for honesty. If you use thee and thou in your prayers, great. And if you stutter or stumble over your words, that's fine too. Do you close your eyes to help you focus? That's great. Pray with eyes open? There's nothing wrong with that. Do you kneel? That's fine. What's most important in prayer is that you speak to God from your heart. Tell God what you're thinking. Tell Him what concerns you have. What dreams you have. What you're thankful for. Pray for yourself, your family, your friends, people you don't know. Pray for colleagues, teachers, pastors, politicians. Don't be afraid to tell God what you're feeling. And don't forget to listen. Prayer isn't simply a one-way street. Always include a time of quiet, a time for listening to God.

What if your heart is hurting or angry or confused? Honest prayers embrace those emotions as readily as they embrace joy, thankfulness, and relief. An honest prayer is an expression of what's on your mind right now.

Perhaps in light of the very personal nature of honest prayer, Jesus also teaches the importance of "going to your closet to pray."

Public prayer has its place—it's an important part of a life of faith—but private prayer is essential. In your closet, it's just you and God. No fancy words needed here.

Your "closet" could be a quiet corner at home where you can pray or a park bench near your place of work. Maybe it's a table at a coffee shop. Perhaps it really is a closet. Choose one or more places you can go that will not only afford you some privacy, but can also become a consistent and familiar praying place. Then be deliberate about going to your private place each day to pray. In that very focused time, you will get to know God and yourself better.

Your closet can also be wherever you are, within yourself. No matter where you find yourself, in whatever circumstance—standing, sitting, kneeling, flat on your back, clinging to a rock—you can silently reach God. Prayer anywhere, anytime is always an option.

By being mindful of God's presence throughout all of your day, you can develop an attitude of prayer. That way, when you face a challenge, discover a need, or hear some great news, you can shoot off a prayer to God no matter what your surroundings. The next time you're back in your prayer closet, you can devote even more time to those concerns or praises.

Pray boldly and often. You won't be marked down for awkward pauses, poor grammatical construction, or unexpected emotional outbursts. God wants to hear your prayers. He wants to hear you express the desires of your heart. He wants you to be you. And He wants to answer those prayers. Pray often. Pray boldly. Then embrace the quiet and listen for God's answers.

I Will

Learn to develop an attitude of prayer.	*yes*	*no*
Know that prayer is simply talking with God.	*yes*	*no*
Desire to spend time alone in prayer every day.	*yes*	*no*
Know that God not only wants to listen to me but to talk to me as well.	*yes*	*no*
Express whatever I'm feeling in my prayer time.	*yes*	*no*
Be confident that my prayers are important to God.	*yes*	*no*
Be aware of where I can enter into prayer privately.	*yes*	*no*

Things to Do

☐ *Ask God to teach you more about prayer.*

☐ *Read Matthew 6:5–13 and examine what this passage says about prayer.*

☐ *Choose a quiet place in your home where you can go to pray in solitude.*

☐ *Ask a pastor for suggestions on how to pray.*

☐ *Take a prayer break instead of one lunch break this week.*

☐ *Create a prayer log that you can use to list prayer concerns or joys.*

☐ *Keep your prayer log current with personal progress notes.*

Things to Remember

Jesus said, "Where two or three are gathered together in My name, I am there in the midst of them."

MATTHEW 18:20 NKJV

This is the confidence that we have in Him, that if we ask anything according to His will, He hears us.

1 JOHN 5:14 NKJV

If you believe, you will receive whatever you ask for in prayer.

MATTHEW 21:22 NKJV

> Jesus said, "Believe that you have received the things you ask for in prayer."
> —Mark 11:24 NCV

Cornelius was a religious man. He and all the other people who lived in his house worshiped the true God. He gave much of his money to the poor and prayed to God often.

ACTS 10:2 NCV

Each morning you listen to my prayer, as I bring my requests to you and wait for your reply.

PSALM 5:3 CEV

We can spend our time praying and
serving God by preaching.

ACTS 6:4 CEV

In return for my love they are my
accusers, but I give myself to prayer.

PSALM 109:4 NKJV

Paul wrote: I want the men everywhere
to pray, lifting up their hands in a holy
manner, without anger and arguments.

1 TIMOTHY 2:8 NCV

He shall pray to God, and He will
delight in him, He shall see His face
with joy, for He restores to man His
righteousness.

JOB 33:26 NKJV

You, beloved, building yourselves up on
your most holy faith, praying in the
Holy Spirit, keep yourselves in the love
of God, looking for the mercy of our
Lord Jesus Christ unto eternal life.

JUDE 20 NKJV

O God, listen to my prayer. Pay
attention to my plea.

PSALM 54:2 NLT

Prayer is a mighty
instrument, not for
getting man's will
done in Heaven,
but for getting
God's will done on
earth.

—ROBERT LAW

Prayer delights
God's ear, it melts
His heart, it opens
His hand: God
cannot deny a
praying soul.

—THOMAS WATSON

Loving Difficult People

Enemy Mine

Jesus said, "You have heard that it was said, 'You shall love your neighbor and hate your enemy.' But I say to you, love your enemies, bless those who curse you, do good to those who hate you, and pray for those who spitefully use you and persecute you."

—*Matthew 5:43–44* NKJV

In most classic works of fiction, the bad guys are pretty easy to discern. They're the people in the dark-colored suits or the dark hats or the characters with the permanent scowls or smirks.

But what about the enemies in real life? In your real life? They may or may not seem quite so devious, but you know who they are. Picture one right now. Then take this challenge: Love that person. Not an easy assignment. Yet Jesus teaches in Matthew that you are to meet that challenge head-on. He said, "Turn hate upside down." It's important to note that Jesus didn't say, "Love evil." He said, "Love people—even those who despise you."

If you have a tough time with this challenge, you're not alone. The people of Jesus' day didn't know what to do with Jesus' love-your-enemies commandment. It's likely that this sort of radical thinking contributed to the eventual backlash that ultimately sent Jesus to the cross. The Jews had been looking for someone who was a dynamic leader—someone who would soundly defeat their enemies. Instead, they got a radical who taught them to "turn the other cheek" and to "love people who hate you."

How can you love someone who hates you? The first step is to recognize that all people are created in God's image. God values every person.

Then try to understand why this person is an enemy. Perhaps he or she person is being malicious, or simply misdirected. Could it be you did something to cause hurt? Seek to know what drives the wedge between you. If it is within your power, do all you can to remove that wedge.

Look for common ground. Enemies are usually formed out of a disagreement in one particular area of life. Put aside that issue for a moment and look for things you can agree on. Focus on these areas in your relationship.

Consider distancing yourself. If there is no reason to be in a relationship with this person, stay away from situations that could be troublesome. Love from a distance is easier that love in the middle of confrontation.

Pray for this person and for wisdom to know how to relate to him or her. Only with a measure of God's love is it possible to love your enemies. God's love can look beyond the hurtful actions and into the possibilities of the heart. It can fill in the gaps in your own ability to love.

I Will

Examine my heart to see if there is any hate in me.

yes   _no_

Trust God to give me an extra helping of love for
those I disdain.

yes   _no_

Know that God's love is big enough even for people I
have a hard time loving.

yes   _no_

Know that I will likely encounter people who seek to
hurt or harm me.

yes   _no_

Keep alert for opportunities to show love to someone
who may be an enemy.

yes   _no_

Prayerfully consider how I should approach those
whom I call enemies.

yes   _no_

Things to Do

☐ _Ask God to fill you with love for difficult people._

☐ _Make a list of people you might call enemies. Pray for each person on
that list._

☐ _Talk with a pastor or trusted friend about your struggles to love
difficult people._

☐ _Discuss with a friend the challenge of loving someone when you don't
condone their actions._

☐ _Come up with one or more ways you can practically show love to an
enemy._

☐ _Write a letter to someone who might be an enemy and express your
love for that person in spite of the circumstances._

Things to Remember

The Lord said: "If your enemy is hungry, feed him; if he is thirsty, give him a drink; for in so doing you will heap coals of fire on his head."

ROMANS 12:20 NKJV

Jesus said, "I say to you who hear: Love your enemies, do good to those who hate you."

LUKE 6:27 NKJV

Don't let evil get the upper hand, but conquer evil by doing good.

ROMANS 12:21 TLB

Jesus said, "Pray for the happiness of those who curse you. Pray for those who hurt you."

LUKE 6:28 NKJV

Jesus said, "If you love those who love you, what reward have you? Do not even the tax collectors do the same?"

MATTHEW 5:46 NKJV

Do not rejoice when your enemy falls, and do not let your heart be glad when he stumbles.

PROVERBS 24:17 NKJV

Where there is no love, pour love in, and you will draw out love.

—SAINT JOHN OF THE CROSS

The first duty of love is to listen.

—PAUL TILLICH

Building Close Relationships

Frequent Flyer Meals

They continued steadfastly in the apostles' doctrine and
fellowship, in the breaking of bread, and in prayers.

—Acts 2:42 NKJV

For an hour or two each week, millions of people participate in church services around the world. Before the services begin, congregation members smile and nod at one another, shake hands, and may even ask "how are you doing?" When the services are over, they smile and nod again, shake hands, and say, "see you next week" before heading off in separate directions. To these people, church is a weekly activity that only rarely intersects with regular life.

In the days of the early church there was little if any distinction between church and regular life. That's because church wasn't a place to go; rather, it was the people with whom you associated in your desire to grow in faith. The early church did this in small groups. They didn't gather just once a week; they gathered and fellowshipped every day and in all aspects of their lives. Descriptions of the early church like the ones found in the book of Acts frequently include the mention of "breaking bread." Breaking bread represented the concept of fellowship, of doing life together.

This idea is just as applicable today. The idea of doing life together is quite simple. It means exploring and applying your faith in community with others. The best way to do this is in a small group (eight to twelve people is just about right). Use your time together to get to know everyone. Share dreams. Tell memories. Study the Bible. Pray. As you get to know each other, celebrate each person's successes. Throw birthday parties or congratulations-on-a-new-job parties. Serve each other's needs in practical ways. Pick up the children of a group member from school or offer a helping hand when a group member is experiencing lean financial times. Most of all, learn to love one another.

If this kind of small group is not available, there are other ways of doing life with your church community. Explore the possibilities of small ministries within the larger ministry of your local church. Consider sharing community with members of your choir, your altar guild, your men's fellowship, your Bible study group, your needleworkers guild, your grounds committee, your church's supper club. The opportunities for living your fellowship by example of the early church are still available and just as valuable today.

In the time you spend with members of your small group, you will discover what it means to do life together. You will get a glimpse of the reason God created you in the first place—to do life with Him.

I Will

Look for opportunities to share life experiences with
friends.   _yes_   _no_

Know that time spent with friends is a key to
growing closer together.   _yes_   _no_

Seek to integrate church life with real life in my
relationships.   _yes_   _no_

Understand that there is some risk involved in doing   _yes_   _no_
life with others.

Desire to grow closer to friends.   _yes_   _no_

Examine my current relationships and see if I can
break bread more often with friends.   _yes_   _no_

Things to Do

 *Plan a get-together with a few friends and talk about what it means to
do life together.*

Throw a celebration for those you wish to know better.

*Choose one or two new people you'd like to know better and invite
them to dinner.*

*Make a list of practical ways to serve people you do life with and then
commit to those actions.*

*Spend a weekend helping a friend with tasks such as cleaning house,
doing laundry, and washing dishes.*

*Invite members of your small group to a movie, play, concert, or other
nonchurch event.*

Things to Remember

All of you be of one mind, having compassion for one another; love as brothers, be tenderhearted, be courteous.

1 PETER 3:8 NKJV

We took sweet counsel together, and walked to the house of God in the throng.

PSALM 55:14 NKJV

Can two walk together, unless they are agreed?

AMOS 3:3 NKJV

Comfort one another.

1 THESSALONIANS 4:18 NKJV

Bear one another's burdens, and in this way you will fulfill the law of Christ.

GALATIANS 6:2 NRSV

All who believed were together, and had all things in common.

ACTS 2:42 NKJV

Paul wrote: I hope to see you on my journey, and to be helped on my way there by you, if first I may enjoy your company for a while.

ROMANS 15:24 NKJV

To live in prayer together is to walk in love together.

—MARGARET MOORE JACOBS

God calls us not to solitary sainthood but to fellowship in a company of committed men.

—DAVID SCHULLER

The Desire for More

I Want One Too

A sound heart is the life of the flesh: but envy the rottenness of the bones.

—*Proverbs 14:30 KJV*

In a world driven by the mentality that more is better, the idea that someone might have something that you don't have can be discomforting. Sure, your house is just fine. It has a warm, lived-in look. But there's just something even more inviting about your friend's new home. If only you had a house like that . . .

If you've ever experienced this feeling, then you've been bitten by envy. Envy is that pervasive and persistent desire for something you don't have but someone else does. That thing could be tangible (like a designer suit, a snappy new sports car, or a well-equipped kitchen) or intangible (like intelligence, leadership ability, poise, or athletic prowess). Envy's tractor beam is sly and powerful—and it is also dangerous. Proverbs calls it "the rottenness of the bones." Any doubt about the writer's feelings toward envy?

What is it about envy that's so terrible? First, envy contaminates contentment. God has promised to take care of you. Are you eating? Good. Have a place to sleep? Excellent. Have clothes on your back and shoes on your feet? Content doesn't hinge on having filet mignon rather than beans or macaroni and cheese. It doesn't hinge on a beautifully appointed home rather than on a small rented mobile home. Contentment comes from a knowledge and satisfaction that your life is good. Wherever you are, there you are. That's what contentment is, and contentment is envy's enemy.

Another danger of envy is that it is a never-ending spiral. There's always a newer, better, faster version of whatever it is you own or want to own, or do or want to do. There's a bigger television. A fancier dining room table. A prettier dress or sharper tie. A more prestigious college. A more impressive job title.

Envy can also build walls. It can separate friends and neighbors into two categories: those who have and those who want what those who have, have. Friendships have been damaged by envy. Families have been destroyed. Tear down those walls by learning to genuinely appreciate the good fortune of others.

One of the best ways to overcome the pull of envy is to actively pursue contentment. Look around at the things you already have. Think of a reason you're thankful for each one: for your home, your friends, your health, your talents. Rediscover the wonder of your good fortune. Enjoy these gifts from God. When you embrace contentment, you not only defeat envy, you also learn how to be happy about what others have. Where envy divides, contentment can build bridges. A content person can honestly be excited with a friend or neighbor about that person's new living room set, DVD player, or laptop computer.

Another way to shun envy is to understand that you don't have to own something in order to appreciate it. Artistic masterpieces are out of financial reach of all but the very wealthy, but you can appreciate their beauty in galleries as much as in your own home. You can enjoy the most brilliant and accomplished orchestras in the world through your area's public radio stations.

Another way to turn down the intensity of envy is to simply avoid putting yourself in its path. Don't go to the auto show if you know you'll just walk away from it feeling like your car isn't good enough. Avoid window-shopping if you have a hard time saying no to new clothes that seem to call out to you by name. Turn off the television for a few days, or at least mute the commercials so you won't be pummeled by its commercial driven you-need-this philosophy.

To fight envy you must also learn to trust that God has your best interests at heart. God has promised to take care of you. That doesn't mean you'll have the best of everything according to this world. God knows what's best for you right now. He knows what He's doing.

Will you ever have a newer house? A nicer car? A better tennis game? A more beautiful smile? Perhaps. And if you do, great! Enjoy. But let God—not Madison Avenue—lead you there. Revel in the life you live today. It's a gift.

Do not envy others—it only leads to harm.
—Psalm 37:8 NLT

I Will

Be open to God revealing to me areas in my life
where I need to be content.   _____ yes   _____ no

Examine my heart and acknowledge any envy I have.   _____ yes   _____ no

Be aware of what kinds of things I envy and learn
why I envy these things.   _____ yes   _____ no

Look for ways to enjoy my current surroundings and
circumstances.   _____ yes   _____ no

Thank God for His provision.   _____ yes   _____ no

Celebrate the good fortune of others without envy.   _____ yes   _____ no

Things to Do

☐ Ask God for contentment.

☐ Make a list of ten gifts God has given you (place to live, food to eat,
family to love, work to do).

☐ Come up with five new ways to enjoy your current circumstances.

☐ Invite a few friends to talk about the danger of envy with you.

☐ Go to a store and look at all the newest products, and then, instead of
buying anything, go home, look around and thank God for all that you
do have.

☐ Turn off the television for a week to avoid the bombardment of you-
need-this advertisements.

☐ Thank God for His provision.

Things to Remember

Seal me in your heart with permanent betrothal, for love is strong as death, and jealousy is as cruel as Sheol. It flashes fire, the very flame of Jehovah.

SONG OF SOLOMON 8:6 TLB

When [Joseph's] brothers saw that their father loved him more than all his brothers, they hated him and could not speak peaceably to him.

GENESIS 37:4 NKJV

> *Let us walk properly, as in the day, not in revelry and drunkenness, not in lewdness and lust, not in strife and envy.*
> —Romans 13:13 NKJV

Wrath is cruel and anger a torrent, but who is able to stand before jealousy?

PROVERBS 27:4 NKJV

In the Parable of the Prodigal Son, Jesus quoted the older son as saying, "All these years I've worked hard for you and never once refused to do a single thing you told me to; and in all that time you never gave me even one young goat for a feast with my friends."

LUKE 15:29 TLB

I saw that for all toil and very skillful work a man is envied by his neighbor. This also is vanity and grasping for the wind.

ECCLESIATES 4:4 NKJV

When Rachel saw that she bore Jacob no children, Rachel envied her sister, and said to Jacob, "Give me children, or else I die!"

GENESIS 30:1 NKJV

Isaac began to prosper, and continued prospering until he became very prosperous; for he had possessions of flocks and possessions of herds and a great number of servants. So the Philistines envied him.

GENESIS 26:13–14 NKJV

Get rid of all malicious behavior and deceit. Don't just pretend to be good! Be done with hypocrisy and jealousy and backstabbing.

1 PETER 2:1 NLT

I envied the proud when I saw them prosper despite their wickedness.

PSALM 73:3 NLT

Envy is rebellion against God's leading in the lives of his children. It's saying that God has no right to bless someone else more than you.

—ERWIN LUTZER

Envy can ruin reputations, split churches, and cause murders. Envy can shrink our circle of friends, ruin our business, and dwarf our souls. . . . I have seen hundreds cursed by it.

—BILLY GRAHAM

Faith and Doubt

Leaping Off Cliffs Blindfolded

What is faith? It is the confident assurance that what we hope for is going to happen. It is the evidence of things we cannot yet see.

—Hebrews 11:1 NLT

Think about the first time you ever doubted. When you began to question the safety of the world around you. When you wondered whether or not you really could succeed at work, school, or even at home. Or when you began to question whether God really did exist. At that very moment, you traded a portion of trust for skepticism. You redefined trust. No longer was your trust blind and unwavering. Instead, it became measured. Caution and fear of disappointment tempered trust.

Anyone who has experienced a broken trust (and that's probably just about everyone) learns the importance of anchoring trust to a tangible, knowable object—to something you can see, touch, taste, smell, or hear. You can trust that a chair will hold your weight because you've sat in chairs before. You can trust that the air will be breathable because it's always been breathable. You can trust that the food you eat will be safe. The electrical outlets, grounded. The car's wheels, firmly attached. You trust close friends because you know them and you know they're for you. You know when it is okay to trust because your skepticism has taught you to always know whom or what you're putting your trust in. But don't let skepticism rule your world. Though trust may come with difficulty at times, it's an important aspect of a healthy life.

Consider faith, trust's older cousin. Faith is an unwavering trust in the existence, omniscience, omnipresence, and omnipotence of God. It is the earnest belief that God really did send his Son to die for your sins and that He loves you. When you encounter an opportunity for faith, all that you've learned about trust becomes meaningless. Faith doesn't fit the mold you've created for trust. Where do you toss the anchor in faith?

Faith requires complete acceptance of the invisible. Faith in God demands belief in something that is beyond belief. Even the Bible recognizes the unique properties of faith. The author of Hebrews used this wonderfully perplexing description: Faith is "the evidence of things we cannot yet see." Wouldn't it be easier if God just knocked on your front door and greeted you face-to-face? Maybe God won't appear on your doorstep, but God does reveal Himself in the Bible. The Bible is your glimpse of both the character of God and of His plan for the world.

Even if you read the Bible a hundred times, however, you're still going to need to forget what you've learned about doubt and distrust if you desire faith. Think of it this way: Faith is jumping off a cliff blindfolded in the black of night and knowing that someone is there catch you. Every time. Even though you've never jumped off that cliff before! Of course, you do know something about where you might land—the Bible promises God will be there for you. Faith is trusting that biblical truth. Only you can discover faith for yourself. A friend can introduce you to God, but that same friend can't hand you a helping of faith. You have to get that for yourself. And here's how: Ask God for it.

Faith doesn't come easily for some. It doesn't come at all for others. Once you've embraced a faith in God, you discover that faith is not static. Your faith can grow. As it does, you can learn to leap from higher places with full confidence that you will land in God's arms (such as following God's will to a new career, sharing your faith boldly with a friend, or giving of your time, talent, or treasure sacrificially).

To grow your faith, get to know God. Read the Bible often. Examine how God worked in history and discover what message His word has for you today. Seek the wise counsel of friends. Join a Bible study or small group if you're not already in one and learn from others' experiences of God. Some people have the gift of faith—seek them out and learn from them. Pray daily for a greater faith. You'll discover in time that your storehouse for faith is far larger than you ever imagined.

There will, however, still be times of doubt. Undoubtedly. You may even have long seasons where doubt reigns. Yet without the possibility of doubt, faith would be meaningless. Hang in there. Keep your eyes open for the evidence of things you cannot see. And when you're ready—maybe even when you're not ready—leap off the cliff again, fully confident of a sure landing place in God's arms.

I Will

Examine and ask God to help me overcome my doubts.

yes _____ no _____

Attempt to understand the Bible's definition of faith.

yes _____ no _____

Consider how much faith I have in God.

yes _____ no _____

Look for ways to increase my measure of faith.

yes _____ no _____

Ask God to teach me about faith.

yes _____ no _____

Learn to have faith in God even when those around me hang onto doubt.

yes _____ no _____

Things to Do

☐ Ask God for a greater reserve of faith.

☐ Write a paragraph detailing the biggest doubts you've had about God. Share this with a trusted friend and talk about your doubts.

☐ Have a friend blindfold you and lead you around your home. Afterward, discuss how trusting your friend to lead you is like and unlike faith that God will lead you.

☐ Interview someone who has doubts about the existence of God.

☐ Read an encyclopedia entry about God to learn about a secular perspective on faith.

☐ Read a book about a well-known Christian and learn about this person's faith.

Things to Remember

With the heart one believes unto righteousness, and with the mouth confession is made unto salvation.

ROMANS 10:10 NKJV

"You didn't have enough faith," Jesus told them. "I assure you, even if you had faith as small as a mustard seed you could say to this mountain, 'Move from here to there,' and it would move. Nothing would be impossible."

MATTHEW 17:20 NLT

Do you see that faith was working together with his works, and by works faith was made perfect?
—James 2:22 NKJV

It is by grace you have been saved, through faith—and this not from yourselves, it is the gift of God.

EPHESIANS 2:8 NIV

Jesus' disciples said, "Now we are sure that You know all things, and have no need that anyone should question You. By this we believe that You came forth from God."

JOHN 16:30 NKJV

In it the righteousness of God is revealed from faith to faith; as it is written, "The just shall live by faith."

ROMANS 1:17 NKJV

I know whom I have believed and am persuaded that He is able to keep what I have committed to Him until that Day.

2 TIMOTHY 1:12 NKJV

I know that my Redeemer lives, and He shall stand at last on the earth.

JOB 19:25 NKJV

Jesus said, "Let not your heart be troubled; you believe in God, believe also in Me."

JOHN 14:1 NKJV

[The signs that Jesus did] are written that you may believe that Jesus is the Christ, the Son of God, and that believing you may have life in His name.

JOHN 20:31 NKJV

The apostles said to the Lord, "Increase our faith."

LUKE 17:5 NKJV

Faith is the Samsonian lock of the Christian; cut it off, and you may put out his eyes—and he can do nothing.

—CHARLES HADDON SPURGEON

[Faith is] the art of holding on to things your reason has once accepted, in spite of your changing moods.

—C. S. LEWIS

Good Works

Did You See That?

Take heed that you do not do your charitable deeds before men, to be seen by them. Otherwise you have no reward from your Father in heaven.

—*Matthew 6:1 NKJV*

When was the last time you were recognized for a good deed? Perhaps a coworker gave you public praise for your assistance on a big project. Maybe a neighbor brought over some cookies as a thank-you for helping her plant a garden. Maybe a family member offered a hug as a reward for your work preparing a meal. Or perhaps a pastor acknowledged you for your tireless volunteer efforts in a charity drive.

It's invigorating to be praised for a good deed. Encouraging words provide fuel for meeting the next challenges. It's great to feel good about doing something of value. Like the praise of others, that good feeling is a here-and-now reward for your deeds.

The Jewish notables in Jesus' day did lots of good works. Many of them were in the good-works business primarily to earn the praise of others. They wanted to hear how good they were, how outstanding their good deeds were. They did good works only for the praise and the good feelings. In doing so, they missed out on another kind of reward—a reward that can be yours, too, with the right heart attitude—praise from God.

Jesus probably stunned his audience when he said that if they were doing good in exchange for applause from others, they shouldn't count on a reward from God. Wow. What a statement. Notice that Jesus did not say that if they couldn't do good without seeking applause, don't do it. He acknowledged that good works are good works no matter what the intent. But He made it perfectly clear that if you do the good works quietly, working for the benefit of others rather than to get a lead story on the five o'clock news, you'll get a unique and particularly personal reward from God. This will come in God's time.

When you do good works, enjoy the good feeling you get. If you also receive the praise of others, relish that too. But always keep your focus on the people you're helping and not on what you hope to gain. Seek your emotional reward from helping a child, doing a good turn for your neighbor, lending a helping hand to a local missions group, visiting older folks whose children may live in another state. You'll get an even greater reward someday from God, which is surely something to look forward to.

I Will

Understand that my real reward for doing good comes from God.

yes   *no*

Seek to do good works for the purpose of helping others.

yes   *no*

Admit that it feels pretty good to be acknowledged for doing good.

yes   *no*

Understand that it's okay not to be noticed for good work I've done.

yes   *no*

Be patient until the day when God rewards my good deeds.

yes   *no*

Thank God for the desire to be charitable toward others.

yes   *no*

Things to Do

- [ ] *Ask God to lead you to opportunities for doing good works.*

- [ ] *Read the book of James to see what the Bible has to say about works and faith.*

- [ ] *List ways in which God might reward you for doing good without expectation of earthly accolades.*

- [ ] *Think of one good deed you can do for a family member or friend without that person knowing. Then do it.*

- [ ] *Contact someone who's done a good deed for you and give praise to him or her.*

- [ ] *Make a mental list of some of your good works and consider how you were (or weren't) recognized for those works.*

Things to Remember

If Abraham was justified by works, he has something to boast about, but not before God.

ROMANS 4:2 NKJV

These things I have told you are all true. Insist on them so that Christians will be careful to do good deeds all the time, for this is not only right, but it brings results.

TITUS 3:8 TLB

We are His workmanship, created in Christ Jesus for good works, which God prepared beforehand that we should walk in them.

EPHESIANS 2:10 NKJV

Remember me, O my God, concerning this, and do not wipe out my good deeds that I have done for the house of my God, and for its services!

NEHEMIAH 13:14 NKJV

Let each one examine his own work, and then he will have rejoicing in himself alone, and not in another.

GALATIANS 6:4 NKJV

It is lamentable, that we should live so long in the world, and do so little for God, or that we should live so short a time in the world, and do so much for Satan.

—THE REVEREND WILLIAM SECKER

Everyone knows that it is much harder to turn word into deed than deed into word.

—MAXIM GORKY

Open Arms

All who believed were together, and had all things in common, and sold their possessions and goods, and divided them among all, as anyone had need.

—*Acts 2:44–45* NKJV

The concept of sharing has been around as long as people have. But in the days of the early church, that concept took on a whole new meaning. Jesus taught that people ought to share willingly with others, not just when it was convenient. He encouraged His followers to take care of "widows and orphans," not only because they couldn't take care of themselves, but also because there is a spiritual benefit to helping. There is a heavenly reward for earthly unselfishness.

It takes a heart motivated by love to give up or share something from the one's possessions. But that is what Jesus taught, and the lesson is as valid today as it was back then. Your possessions include everything that you own, all your material goods—lawn mower, car, kitchen appliances, dishes, books, clothes, furniture, even money. But your possessions also include such valuable commodities as time, talent, and attention.

Sharing your possessions with others often requires

sacrifice, but God doesn't ask that you give indiscriminately. The first group of people you should reach out to are those with whom you do life—your family, friends, small group members. Then, consider giving to just about anyone else with a need.

Before you give things away, however, examine the need. Is the person unable to meet that need by himself or herself? Will your assistance improve the person's situation, or will it perpetuate an unhealthy habit? If by reaching out you can make a positive difference, it is probably what you should do. Sometimes, though, you won't be able to effectively assess the validity of a need. That's okay. It may be worth the risk. Ask God to help you make a good decision, and then do it.

Perhaps you know a skill that can help out a neighbor. Can you fix a leaky faucet? Paint window trim? Format a computer's hard drive? Maybe you can give the gift of time. Do you know a friend who is hurting? Your patient, listening ear can be a tremendous gift. Or perhaps you can share your material goods. A family with a suddenly reduced income may appreciate your gift of food, clothing, or even some money to help with bills. The better you know the people you care about, the more readily and effectively you'll be able to reach out in times of need.

Jesus said that whatever you do to help others, you are also doing for Him. Sure makes reaching out a lot easier, doesn't it?

I Will

Know that there is a spiritual reward for reaching out to others.   *yes*   *no*

Consider all the times someone has reached out to me and be thankful.   *yes*   *no*

Consider what it means to be willing to share.   *yes*   *no*

Share from my resources willingly.   *yes*   *no*

Look for opportunities to reach out to others.   *yes*   *no*

Evaluate my level of selfishness.   *yes*   *no*

Know that it's normal to sometimes feel a little selfish.   *yes*   *no*

Things to Do

☐ *Ask God to give you an unselfish spirit.*

☐ *Contact a local charity and ask what the current greatest needs are. Give what you can to help meet those needs.*

☐ *Take stock of your material goods and come up with three ways you can use these items to help someone you know.*

☐ *Clean out your garage or attic and donate as much stuff as possible to a local organization such as Goodwill or The Salvation Army.*

☐ *Give up an activity you enjoy (such as watching a favorite television show or reading the newspaper) and use the time instead to talk with a needy friend or neighbor.*

Things to Remember

Whoever has this world's goods, and sees his brother in need, and shuts up his heart from him, how does the love of God abide in him?

1 JOHN 3:17 NKJV

Zacchaeus stood and said to the Lord, "Look, Lord, I give half of my goods to the poor; and if I have taken anything from anyone by false accusation, I restore fourfold."

LUKE 19:8 NKJV

God is fair; he will not forget the work you did and the love you showed for him by helping his people. And he will remember that you are still helping them.

HEBREWS 6:10 NCV

Jesus said, "Use worldly wealth to gain friends for yourselves, so that when it is gone, you will be welcomed into eternal dwellings."

LUKE 16:9 NIV

He who sows sparingly will also reap sparingly, and he who sows bountifully will also reap bountifully.

2 CORINTHIANS 9:6 NKJV

God has given us two hands—one for receiving and the other for giving.

—BILLY GRAHAM

We must not only give what we have; we must also give what we are.

—DÉSIRÉ JOSEPH MERCIER

Experiencing Joy

More Than a Dance of Raindrops

At midnight Paul and Silas prayed, and sang praises unto God: and the prisoners heard them.

—ACTS 16:25 KJV

Moments of joy are powerful whether they come in a sprinkle or a torrent. Perhaps you've experienced joy in the unexpected giggle of a toddler, in a sudden breeze that brings you the smell of a mossy stream bank, or in the streak of a shooting star across a clear night sky. Joy like this is treasured because it is rare and transcendent. It reaches beyond practicality and expectation and touches a profound place in your soul.

Moments of joy are magnificent. But there is a deeper kind of joy. This joy is deeply fulfilling and so much bigger than the warm feeling you get while watching dancing raindrops on a windowpane. It is a joy that stays with you even in times of great difficulty.

Paul knew this kind of joy. It's what gave him the strength to sing praises to God while in jail. With great joy, Paul and his friend Silas praised God together behind bars. They were so exuberant in their joy, in fact, that their voices carried to other prisoners' cells. Had Paul lost his mind? What in the world could he have been joyful about while in jail? Paul's joy came not from his surroundings or circumstance, but from his delight in God. It came from knowing that he was in the center of God's will. It's relatively easy to find pockets of joy as you observe creation in all its glory, but when your joy is anchored in God, it can infuse all aspects of your life.

The first step to knowing this kind of joy is to recognize that God is with you, no matter what happens or where you are. God is always near. Or you can think of it this way: The Creator of the universe cares about you so much that He is a constant companion. There is a certain joy in this knowledge alone—God desires to be near you, not because He wants to point out your faults, but because He longs to make your life rich and full.

The second step is to acknowledge that God knows what He's doing (even if it doesn't make sense to you at the time). Sometimes this is going to be a real challenge, but it's critically important if you desire to know true joy. You know from experience that when you delight in God, tears and pain don't magically go away. You're still going to go through tough times. Know that God has a solid grasp on the big picture, even though from your perspective things may not look all that great. God's plan is a good one. You can know deep, abiding joy by learning to trust in God's plan. God is in control.

The third step is to search for God's will—the path He desires you to take in life. Through Bible study and prayer, you can begin to piece together some of the puzzle that is God's will. Wise counsel from a pastor or friends can help too. The more you get to know God, the more you can know His will. And the more you know God's will and follow it, the more you will be like Paul, rejoicing no matter what the circumstance because you know you're right where God wants you to be.

Finally, consider what God did for you when He sent Jesus to die on the cross: He removed your sin and gave you a new life—a life that ultimately leads to heaven. While the image of Jesus on the cross is certainly sobering for its achingly real picture of suffering, it truly represents a reason to rejoice: God loves you that much. He desires a relationship with you. He wants to give you eternal life. Think about that for a moment. Joy wells up inside when you truly begin to comprehend the sacrifice God made in order to bring you into relationship with Him.

Wouldn't you like to discover joy in the middle of a work crisis? Or joy in the middle of a relational disaster? The tastes of joy you experience as life unfolds around you are God-given and tantalizing, but they are only temporary. Joy in knowing and delighting in God, however, is both accessible and limitless.

> My people will be happy forever
> because of the things I will make.
> I will make a Jerusalem that is full of joy,
> and I will make her people a delight.
> —ISAIAH 65:18 NCV

I Will

Seek God's will so I may know joy.   *yes*   *no*

Learn to delight in God no matter what my
circumstances.   *yes*   *no*

Enjoy the tastes of joy I experienced as a child.   *yes*   *no*

Trust that God is always near.   *yes*   *no*

Know that a deep joy is available even if I don't have
a lot of happy memories.   *yes*   *no*

Look for ways to share about the source of my joy with
others.   *yes*   *no*

Things to Do

☐ *Make a list describing times you discovered joy when life was tough.*

☐ *Call a friend and ask what brings him or her the most joy.*

☐ *Write DELIGHT IN GOD on a note card and display it in a prominent place at home.*

☐ *Write a description of the source of your joy on a sheet of paper and reflect on those words.*

☐ *Read 1 John 1:1–4 and reflect on what it means to be "full of joy."*

☐ *Ask a friend or family member how he or she has experienced the joy of knowing God.*

Things to Remember

Break forth into joy, sing together, you waste places of Jerusalem! For the Lord has comforted His people, He has redeemed Jerusalem.

ISAIAH 52:9 NKJV

The time will come when God's redeemed will all come home again. They shall come with singing to Jerusalem, filled with joy and everlasting gladness; sorrow and mourning will all disappear.

ISAIAH 51:11 TLB

These things we write to you that your joy may be full.
—1 John 1:4 NKJV

Although you have not seen him, you love him; and even though you do not see him now, you believe in him and rejoice with an indescribable and glorious joy.

1 PETER 1:8 NRSV

Your words were found, and I ate them, and Your word was to me the joy and rejoicing of my heart; for I am called by Your name, O Lord God of hosts.

JEREMIAH 15:16 NKJV

Nevertheless do not rejoice in this, that the spirits are subject to you, but rather rejoice because your names are written in heaven.

LUKE 10:20 NKJV

The LORD is my strength and my shield; my heart trusted in Him, and I am helped; therefore my heart greatly rejoices, and with my song I will praise Him.

PSALM 28:7 NKJV

The LORD has done great things for us, and we are glad.

PSALM 126:3 NKJV

My people will be happy forever because of the things I will make. I will make a Jerusalem that is full of joy, and I will make her people a delight.

ISAIAH 65:18 NCV

I will go to the altar of God, to God my exceeding joy; and on the harp I will praise You, O God, my God.

PSALM 43:4 NKJV

Rejoice always.

1 THESSALONIANS 5:16 NKJV

Conquering any difficulty always gives one a secret joy, for it means pushing back a boundary-line and adding to one's liberty.

—HENRI FRÉDÉRIC AMIEL

The joy that comes past hope and beyond expectation is like no other pleasure in extent.

—SOPHOCLES

God's Word

Open-Book Test

Happy are people of integrity, who follow the law of the LORD. Happy are those who obey his decrees and search for him with all their hearts.

—*Psalm 119:1–2* NLT

God makes it known that the Bible is pretty important reading material in a number of different ways: directly through passages like that in Psalm 119:1–2; indirectly through Jesus' frequent references to Old Testament writings during his earthly ministry; and also through the guiding of His Spirit. But while the Bible is the best-selling book of all time, it may just have one of the lowest reading-to-owning ratios.

In part, that may be because the Bible can be a bit intimidating. Not only is it a lot of material to get a handle on, but it also holds the key to knowing God. Through the history, wisdom, stories, and letters in the Bible, God gives its readers a window to His nature as well as a guidebook for life.

Though you can read through the Bible like a novel, cover to cover, the best way to approach the Bible may be to read sections that apply to a current need or life situation. Many Bibles—especially study Bibles and devotional Bibles—offer helpful topical information that can direct you to other passages that deal with the same subjects. Many of these Bibles have a day-by-day plan that outlines a reading schedule that allows you to read the entire Bible through in a year or two (in a nonsequential, but logical manner). Or you can dive into one of the books and focus solely on that. The Gospel of John is a great place to learn about God's love. If you're looking for wisdom, check out Proverbs.

Unlike some books you read once and never pick up again, the Bible offers new insights every time you read it. Scholars who have studied the Bible all their lives continue to uncover truth and wisdom when they read the Scriptures. One of the greatest things about the Bible is that most of your life's tests are open-book tests, that is, you are free to explore and learn from the Bible whenever there is a need.

But don't wait for a need before cracking open your Bible. The more you study and read, the more you'll uncover about how to live a life of faith. God knows that His word is good for you. That's why He wants you to read it. Often. He wants you to wrestle with the tough parts. He wants you to embrace the aha! discoveries with passion. Most of all, He wants you to get to know Him better.

I Will

Know that God wants me to read the Bible.

yes _no_

Get to know God better by reading the Bible.

yes _no_

Expect to be overwhelmed at times by the scope of the Bible.

yes _no_

Trust that God will show me His will in part through the Bible.

yes _no_

Look for insight and wisdom for life in the Bible.

yes _no_

Know that each time I read the Bible I can come away with new insights.

yes _no_

Pray that God would reveal Himself and His will through the Bible.

yes _no_

Things to Do

☐ _If you're not already in one, join a Bible study that requires weekly Bible-reading homework._

☐ _Read the Gospel of John._

☐ _Study the book of Proverbs and record your insights on a sheet of paper or in a notebook._

☐ _Call a pastor or other church leader and ask for help with a difficult-to-understand Bible passage._

☐ _Choose a verse that's meaningful to you and memorize it._

☐ _Make a list of Bible passages that you have difficulty understanding. Invite a group of friends or church leaders to discuss these with you._

Things to Remember

As newborn babies want milk, you should want the pure and simple teaching. By it you can grow up and be saved.

1 PETER 2:2 NCV

"Is not My word like a fire?" says the LORD, "and like a hammer that breaks the rock in pieces?"

JEREMIAH 23:29 NKJV

Direct my steps by Your word, and let no iniquity have dominion over me.

PSALM 119:133 NKJV

Be diligent to present yourself approved to God, a worker who does not need to be ashamed, rightly dividing the word of truth.

2 TIMOTHY 2:15 NKJV

The word of God is living and powerful and sharper than any two-edged sword, piercing even to the division of soul and spirit, and of joints and marrow, and is a discerner of the thoughts and intents of the heart.

HEBREWS 4:12 NKJV

Jesus said, "All who reject me and my message will be judged at the Day of Judgment by the truths I have spoken."

JOHN 12:48 TLB

If we understood what happens when we use the Word of God, we would use it oftener.

—OSWALD CHAMBERS

The Bible is alive, it speaks to me; it has feet, it runs after me; it has hands, it lays hold on me.

—MARTIN LUTHER

Assurance

Know that You Know

I have written this to you who believe in the Son of God so that you may know you have eternal life.

—*1 John 5:13* TLB

For all of its contextual power, promise is really a delicate word. Just ask anyone who's ever been told "I promise I'll be there for you," only to stare after disappearing taillights during a moment of need. Or ask a child who, even though his soccer game has ended, is still stealing glances at the empty sidelines where his mother or father had promised to be.

Wariness about the security and trustworthiness of promises sneaks into all kinds of relationships. For those who love God, that wariness can eat away at the most basic aspect of faith: assurance that you really have been saved, that eternal life is yours. God promises eternal life to all those who accept Jesus and follow Him. But if your experience with earthly promises is anything to go by, that may seem like a fragile proposition. You may even wonder if you need to have repeat conversion experiences to be assured of a relationship with God.

The congregation John wrote to in 1 John was

probably dealing with this very issue. The entire fifth chapter deals with issues of assurance: assurance that all who know Christ are truly Christians, assurance that God does answer prayer, and assurance in eternal life. Here's what Paul said to that congregation: God does what He says He's going to do. Once you've entered God's kingdom, you're in. It's a done deal. Heaven is a given for all who follow Christ.

This is great news. In a world where assurance is as slippery as an icy sidewalk, having assurance in your relationship with God can be just the anchor you need to weave through life's many disappointments.

Still, the human qualities of doubt and distrust can eat away at your assurance. To gird your assurance, read what the Bible teaches about assurance (Ephesians 3:12 and Romans 10:9, for starters). Then listen to God's Spirit. God's Spirit can offer comfort and confidence about your status with God. Finally, pray. Ask God directly and specifically for assurance in your relationship with Him.

If you've accepted Christ, you already have the key to eternal life. God handed it to you when you reached out to Him. This key is not some temporary, fleeting promise that can be yanked away on a whim. It's real, solid, and lasts a lifetime. When you embrace the trustworthiness of God's promises for those who love Him, you'll be able to simply state, "I know that I know." And that will be enough.

I Will

Know that God's promise of eternal life is assured for
those who accept Christ.   *yes*   *no*
                                                          _____   _____

Pray for assurance if my confidence wanes.   *yes*   *no*
                                                          _____   _____

Use the assurance of God's promises as an anchor for
times when earthly promises fail.   *yes*   *no*
                                                          _____   _____

Share my confidence with others who struggle with
assurance.   *yes*   *no*
                                                          _____   _____

Work toward keeping all the promises I make.   *yes*   *no*
                                                          _____   _____

Carefully consider any promises I make to others.   *yes*   *no*
                                                          _____   _____

Investigate what the Bible teaches about the
assurance of eternal life.   *yes*   *no*
                                                          _____   _____

Things to Do

☐ *Ask God for your own confidence in God's promises.*

☐ *Read 1 John 5 and examine what John has to say about assurance.*

☐ *Have coffee with a pastor and talk about the doubts you've experienced with the promise of eternal life.*

☐ *Review the promises that you've made and have broken, then make a plan for keeping promises in the future.*

☐ *Read about the life of a well-known Christian, looking specifically for that person's experience with doubt and assurance.*

☐ *List five things you are sure about in life. Compare these to what you believe about the assurance of eternal life.*

Things to Remember

We give thanks to God always for you all, making mention of you in our prayers . . . knowing, beloved brethren, your election by God.

1 THESSALONIANS 1:2, 4 NKJV

Jesus said, "He who hears My word and believes in Him who sent Me has everlasting life, and shall not come into judgment, but has passed from death into life."

JOHN 5:24 NKJV

You will be saved, if you honestly say, "Jesus is Lord," and if you believe with all your heart that God raised him from death.

ROMANS 10:9 CEV

Jesus said, "I give them eternal life, and they shall never perish; neither shall anyone snatch them out of My hand."

JOHN 10:28 NKJV

We can come fearlessly right into God's presence, assured of his glad welcome when we come with Christ and trust him.

EPHESIANS 3:12 TLB

Our confidence in Christ does not make us lazy, negligent, or careless, but on the contrary it awakens us, urges us on, and makes us active in living righteous lives and doing good.

—ULRICH ZWINGLI

Confidence is a plant of slow growth.

—ENGLISH PROVERB

A Way Out

No temptation has overtaken you except such as is common to man; but God is faithful, who will not allow you to be tempted beyond what you are able, but with the temptation will also make the way of escape.

—*1 Corinthians 10:13* NKJV

In a society where people are propelled onward by the concept of more, more, and still more, excess rules. The temptation to eat one more cookie, buy one more CD; watch one more movie is strong. The temptation to flirt anonymously over the Internet, to take an extra half-hour for lunch, to sleep in when you promised to help your neighbor set up for the yard sale . . . Giving in to temptation often wins out over more prudent (and many times, healthier) choices.

Temptations are all around you. Sometimes they're easy to ignore, but usually they attract like magnets. Paul made a bold statement, quoted above, about temptation in his first letter to the Corinthian church. He said that God always gives a way out of temptation.

Notice that he didn't say God would erase all

temptation from your life. Nope. Temptation is pretty much a given. Sometimes you'll experience it at the buffet line (where your health and waistline are at risk), and other times you'll meet it in the particularly striking profile of a friendly coworker (where your entire family is at risk).

The first step to overcoming temptation is to recognize it. Do you feel compelled to do something you're not sure is a good idea? That's the tug of temptation. Temptation often comes disguised as a shortcut. It promises an easier path to a desired result, but conveniently forgets to mention that the path is figuratively littered with broken glass, potholes, and land mines.

The second step is to listen to your conscience. When you feel that you are being tempted, the hesitation you sense is a warning. It's an opportunity to uncover the lie that informs temptation. It's an opportunity to evade being taken in.

The third step is to weigh the consequences of your decision. Being tempted to eat a second cookie might not have terrible repercussions if you usually don't overeat, but cheating on your taxes or spouse undoubtedly would. As much as possible, avoid situations where you know you could be tempted. Sometimes, just following your intuition and staying away is God's promised way out.

Recognition, conscience, consequences—and prayer. Whenever you feel temptation's tug, pray. Ask God for wisdom. Ask God for strength to face the temptation. God promised not to set any temptation before you that you can't handle. God will give you the strength you need to handle temptation.

I Will

Ask God to help me overcome temptations.

yes   *no*

Know that I will face temptation often.

yes   *no*

Listen to what my conscience tells me about
tempting circumstances.

yes   *no*

Be confident that I can overcome temptation.

yes   *no*

Attempt to identify potentially tempting situations in
order to avoid them as much as possible.

yes   *no*

Weigh the consequences of giving in to temptation.

yes   *no*

Know that giving in to temptation can sometimes be
devastating.

yes   *no*

Things to Do

☐ *Ask God for wisdom to always see the way out of temptation.*

☐ *Review a recent temptation you gave in to and determine what way
out you may have ignored or missed.*

☐ *Invite a friend to lunch and ask him or her for advice on handling
temptation.*

☐ *Read Matthew 4:1–11 and examine how Jesus dealt with temptation.*

☐ *Determine one activity you should stop or alter so you aren't put into
the path of temptation.*

☐ *List five things that you're often tempted by. Determine ways to avoid
each temptation.*

Things to Remember

Jesus said, "Stay awake and pray for strength against temptation. The spirit wants to do what is right, but the body is weak."

MATTHEW 26:41 NCV

This High Priest of ours understands our weaknesses since he had the same temptations we do, though he never once gave way to them and sinned.

HEBREWS 4:15 TLB

The LORD said to Satan, "Have you considered My servant Job, that there is none like him on the earth, a blameless and upright man, one who fears God and shuns evil? And still he holds fast to his integrity."

JOB 2:3 NKJV

Watch, stand fast in the faith, be brave, be strong.

1 CORINTHIANS 16:13 NKJV

The righteous should choose his friends carefully, for the way of the wicked leads them astray.

PROVERBS 12:26 NKJV

You are of God, little children, and have overcome them, because He who is in you is greater than he who is in the world.

1 JOHN 4:4 NKJV

Call on God, but row away from the rocks.

—RALPH WALDO EMERSON

Every temptation is an opportunity for us to draw nearer to God.

—GEORGE SWEETING

Humility

Where Credit Is Due

Jesus said, "Whoever humbles himself as this little child is the greatest in the kingdom of heaven."

—*Matthew 18:4* NKJV

"Look what I did! Look at me!" Are these the happy words of a youngster who just built a tower out of blocks or climbed to the top of a jungle gym for the first time? Perhaps. But these words could also come from the lips of many adults. Only from an adult, the words often carry a different meaning. They convey pride instead of delight; they embody self-congratulation instead of surprise.

You've heard the biblical proverb, "Pride goes before destruction, and a haughty spirit before a fall," right? Pride can be a negative thing. But what is the alternative? How should you relate to others (especially when you've done something worth noting)? Put on humility.

When Jesus said that the "meek will inherit the earth," He wasn't suggesting that the meek would someday rise up and clobber those who choose the spotlight of self-congratulation. Instead, he was simply acknowledging the incredible strength that comes from honoring God above self. That's what humility is all about. It's a spiritual issue and not just an issue of personality or character trait. Both in-your-face, driven leaders and soft-spoken followers can learn humility.

Being humble means giving God credit for what God has done. God gave you the ability to help others. So when you have the opportunity to make a difference, God should get the kudos. Being humble also means doing good for good's sake rather than for your own gain.

Practice thinking of others more highly than yourself. Humility turns the tables on the it's-all-about-me philosophy and reworks it to an it's-all-about-you philosophy. To be truly humble, forget about seeking the spotlight and instead be content helping others even though God may be only one witness to your actions.

Learn to find your significance in your actions or deeds rather than in the acknowledgment for those actions or deeds. Instead of helping a friend because you know that friend will speak highly of you to others, help your friend because you find joy in helping. It's perfectly fine to enjoy doing something of worth. Allow that to be enough.

Humility is rarely applauded in today's society, but that's not such a big loss. The congratulatory words of colleagues and friends pale in comparison to the rewards offered by the Creator of the universe. God promises a heavenly reward for living humbly. God's spotlight shines far brighter than anything humans can come up with.

I Will

Know that God honors a humble spirit.

yes _____   no _____

Consider if I am seeking an inappropriate spotlight
for things I've done.

yes _____   no _____

Endeavor to understand what true humility is.

yes _____   no _____

Acknowledge God's role in the good things I
accomplish.

yes _____   no _____

Approach God with humility.

yes _____   no _____

Know that heavenly rewards are far greater than
earthly applause.

yes _____   no _____

Learn to act with humility in all of life's
circumstances.

yes _____   no _____

Things to Do

☐ Ask a trusted friend to give you an honest evaluation of your humility.

☐ Determine something you can do for another person without that
person knowing. Afterward, enjoy the thought of God's smile for your
secret act.

☐ Make a list of the things you do that cause you to seek the spotlight.
Consider ways to approach each thing with humility instead.

☐ Watch a popular television situation comedy with a friend. Afterward,
discuss how the characters did or did not express humility.

☐ Seek out someone you believe is good at living out the ideal of
humility, and talk with this person about the joys and challenges of
humility.

Things to Remember

As God's chosen people, holy and dearly loved, clothe yourselves with compassion, kindness, humility, gentleness, and patience.

COLOSSIANS 3:12 NIV

God resists the proud, but gives grace to the humble.

1 PETER 5:5 NKJV

Let no one cheat you of your reward, taking delight in false humility and worship of angels, intruding into those things which he has not seen, vainly puffed up by his fleshly mind.

COLOSSIANS 2:18 NKJV

Get down on your knees before the master; it's the only way you'll ever get on your feet.

JAMES 4:10 THE MESSAGE

True humility and respect for the Lord lead a man to riches, honor, and long life.

PROVERBS 22:4 NKJV

Blessed are the meek, for they shall inherit the earth.

MATTHEW 5:5 NKJV

Genuine humility is unconscious . . . God's workmen must be so emptied of self that they are unconsciously humble.

—WATCHMAN NEE

Humility does not consist simply in thinking cheaply of oneself, so much as in not thinking of oneself at all—and of Christ more and more.

—KEITH BROOKS

Wisdom

Hold the Gold, Please

My instruction is far more valuable than silver or gold. For the value of wisdom is far above rubies; nothing can be compared with it.

—Proverbs 8:10–11 TLB

Behind door number one is a wheelbarrow full of gold (go ahead and imagine it as big as you like). Behind door number two is an opportunity to gain wisdom. You can only open one door. Which would you choose? (Here's a not-so-subtle hint: Go for the wisdom.)

According to Proverbs, wisdom's value is far greater than a wheelbarrow full of gold or rubies or hundred-dollar bills. If that seems odd to you, you're not alone. Just ask a few people this question, "What is the one thing you wish you had more of in life?" More often than not the answer will be "money," with "time" coming in a close second. (And what is time anyway? That's right—money.) You're not likely to hear the answer "wisdom" all that often.

Why does the author of Proverbs place such a high value on wisdom? In part because wisdom is so much bigger than wealth. While money can get you more and better stuff, wisdom can enrich all aspects of your life. In addition, wisdom is a worthy pursuit because God wants you to seek it.

It is important to note that there is a difference between knowledge and wisdom. Knowledge is simply what you know. Knowledge is what school taught you—facts, details, information, trivia. You can have a whole lot of knowledge and still be unwise. Wisdom is knowing what to do with knowledge. Wisdom is knowing the right decision to make when the choices aren't clear. According to the Bible, the pursuit of wisdom should be the greatest pursuit, next to a relationship with Christ.

Biblical wisdom is also the path to understanding the human condition, the path to understanding life, and the path to understanding God. The greater the wisdom, the greater your opportunity for living life to its fullest.

At this point, the choice between dollars and wisdom probably seems like a no-brainer. Of course you want wisdom. But how do you get it?

Acquiring wisdom begins with desire. You must want to become wise. Sounds simple enough, but many people are perfectly content to seek immediate rewards rather than the long-term benefits of wisdom. They'd rather grab all the cash they can hold than cultivate wisdom they can't even see. However, these people are missing out on an important truth: Riches can't make a person wise, but wisdom can make a person rich.

After desire comes study. A solid foundation of knowledge can go a long way toward growing wisdom. What should you study? The Bible, primarily. It is packed with wise advice (especially in the book of Proverbs) and teachings on wisdom.

The more you get to know God's Word, the more wisdom you'll gain in spiritual things.

Your study time should also include Bible commentaries, which are Bible scholars' interpretations of Scripture. Read the works of great Christian writers, too, such as C. S. Lewis and Charles Spurgeon. Soak up as much wisdom as possible from those people who have already examined the many aspects of faith. Their wisdom can be just as valuable in your life too.

After study comes dialogue. Talk with pastors, church leaders, and other Christians. A Bible study group can be a wonderful place to increase wisdom. By bouncing ideas off other people, you can discover new insights into God's Word and into the nature of God.

And after dialogue comes life experience. Live deliberately with eyes wide open. Much wisdom comes through the experiences of life. If you approach each day with a desire to learn and understand, you'll have plenty of opportunities to develop wisdom.

Ask God for wisdom. Ask Him to reveal new truths as you study the Bible, read scholars' works, dialogue with others, and experience life. You'll be amazed at the surprising truths that come simply by asking God for more wisdom.

Finally, be patient. While you may be able to cram at the last minute for a test at school, there is no shortcut to wisdom. It takes time to develop. Use all the avenues open to you, and invest yourself in the lifetime pursuit of wisdom and you'll reap the rewards each day as you learn to live a full, rich life of faith.

I Will

Consider the importance I place on becoming rich.   *yes* *no*

Seek to understand the value of wisdom.   *yes* *no*

Learn to pursue wisdom over riches.   *yes* *no*

Read the Bible often so I can to grow in wisdom.

Learn from experiences in order to add to wisdom.   *yes* *no*

Learn what I can from others who are wise.   *yes* *no*

Be patient in my pursuits.   *yes* *no*

Things to Do

☐ *Ask God for wisdom.*

☐ *Read from the book of Proverbs and learn about the importance of wisdom.*

☐ *Seek out someone you consider to be wise and spend time talking with that person about the value of wisdom.*

☐ *Watch a popular television drama. Discuss with a friend what the characters seem to value most. What role (if any) does wisdom play in their lives?*

☐ *Write your own poem or proverb describing your desire for wisdom.*

☐ *Invite a few friends over to discuss practical ways to grow wisdom.*

☐ *Review past unwise choices you've made and determine how your experiences have made you wiser.*

Things to Remember

Get the truth and don't ever sell it; also get wisdom, discipline, and discernment.

PROVERBS 23:22 NLT

Wisdom and knowledge will be the stability of your times, and the strength of salvation.

ISAIAH 33:6 NKJV

Wisdom is like money: they both help. But wisdom is better, because it can save whoever has it.

ECCLESIASTES 7:12 NCV

Happy is the man who finds wisdom, and the man who gains understanding.
—Proverbs 3:13 NKJV

The wisdom that is from above is first pure, then peaceable, gentle, willing to yield, full of mercy and good fruits, without partiality and without hypocrisy.

JAMES 3:17 NKJV

The LORD gives wisdom; from His mouth come knowledge and understanding.

PROVERBS 2:6 NKJV

Think over these three illustrations, and
may the Lord help you to understand
how they apply to you.

2 TIMOTHY 2:7 TLB

If any of you lacks wisdom, let him ask
of God, who gives to all liberally and
without reproach, and it will be given to
him.

JAMES 1:5 NKJV

Great is our LORD, and mighty in power;
His understanding is infinite.

PSALM 147:5 NKJV

I will give you a mouth and wisdom
which all your adversaries will not be
able to contradict or resist.

LUKE 21:15 NKJV

If you love Wisdom and don't reject her,
she will watch over you.

PROVERBS 4:6 CEV

Teach us to number our days, that we
may gain a heart of wisdom.

PSALM 90:12 NKJV

Wisdom is, in fact,
the practical side
of moral goodness.

—J. I. PACKER

[Biblical] wisdom
is always
associated with
righteousness and
humility and is
never found apart
from godliness and
true holiness of
life.

—A. W. TOZER

Your Piece of the Puzzle

If it is possible, as much as depends on you, live peaceably with all men.

—Romans 12:18 NKJV

What is your picture of peace? It may be getting away to a quiet weekend at a bed and breakfast. It could be settling down into a comfortable chair to read a book. Perhaps it's that moment when all the family members but you have gone to bed and the only noise you hear is the crackling of a fireplace while you sip coffee or tea.

Notice anything similar about these pictures? Most of them are experienced alone. The picture of peace many people come up with is often a variation on the peace-and-quiet ideal. Peace is easy when there's no one else involved.

When two or more people are together, however, peace can be a real challenge. This is perhaps most evident in the wars that rage across the globe. But it's also evident closer to home. It's a given in life that you won't always get along with everyone you encounter (that includes family members as well as friends). Sometimes people will just get on your nerves. Other times, they will confront you with a challenge. A few will even single you out for an argument.

Learning to be at peace when you are with others begins with patience. Not everyone moves at the same pace. Many confrontations can be sidestepped simply by allowing time for more discussion, time for the rest of the story to play out.

Being at peace with others is also made easier when you have both self-confidence and an open mind. Self-confidence can help you maintain control while you listen to the potentially challenging word of others. Bringing an open mind into conversations helps to break down stubborn walls that inhibit peaceful exchange. Make the goal of your dialogue to understand your coworker, family member, or friend, and you'll be able to live in peace with that person.

Paul's command to live at peace with everyone comes with a carefully worded qualification: "If it is possible, as much as depends on you." All you can do is control your own words and actions. You can seek to understand the other person first instead of immediately responding with your opinion or idea, but you can't control that person's response.

Finally, know that you can always find peace in your relationship with Christ. Just as Jesus calmed the raging seas so the disciples would not be afraid, He can calm your troubled relational waters. Draw comfort and serenity from this.

I Will

Learn from Jesus' example how to be a peacemaker
in difficult situations.

yes   no

Know that God can teach me how to be at peace
with others.

yes   no

Evaluate how well I seek peace in relationships.

yes   no

Define what it means to be a peacemaker in
everyday situations.

yes   no

Look for ways to avoid unnecessary conflicts.

yes   no

Know that I can't force others to be at peace
with me.

yes   no

Things to Do

☐ Ask God to reveal to you what it means to live in peace with others.

☐ Look through a history book and identify what may have prompted the
start of a military conflict such as the Revolutionary War, World War I
or II, or the Vietnam conflict.

☐ Talk to the most at-peace-with-everyone person you know to learn
about what it takes to be a peacemaker.

☐ Seek a peaceful solution to a conflict you've recently experienced with
another person.

☐ Evaluate a recent situation where you did a good job of seeking peace.
What can you learn from this situation to help you with future
conflicts?

Things to Remember

Be of good comfort, be of one mind, live in peace; and the God of love and peace will be with you.

2 CORINTHIANS 13:11 NKJV

Flee also youthful lusts; but pursue righteousness, faith, love, peace with those who call on the Lord out of a pure heart.

2 TIMOTHY 2:22 NKJV

He will give his people strength. He will bless them with peace.

PSALM 29:11 TLB

Therefore, having been justified by faith, we have peace with God through our Lord Jesus Christ.

ROMANS 5:1 NKJV

At day's end I'm ready for sound sleep, for you, God, have put my life back together.

PSALM 4:8 THE MESSAGE

Jesus said, "These things I have spoken to you, that in Me you may have peace. In the world you will have tribulation; but be of good cheer, I have overcome the world."

JOHN 16:33 NKJV

The peace of God is that eternal calm which lies far too deep in the praying, trusting soul to be reached by any external disturbances.

—A. T. PIERSON

When Christ came into the world, peace was sung; and when He went out of the world, peace was bequeathed.

—FRANCIS BACON

God's Timing

A Different Zone

He purposed in Himself, that in the dispensation of the fullness of the times He might gather together in one all things in Christ, both which are in heaven and which are on earth—in Him.

—*Ephesians 1:10* NKJV

Whether you're a cog in a corporate wheel who spends most of the day keeping a dozen plates spinning, a stay-at-home parent juggling your children's schedules as well as your own, or a student micromanaging a pile of classroom books that exceeds your backpack's daily capacity, you're at the mercy of time's relentless insistence to press on.

There's no stopping time. Perhaps that's why it's so frustrating when things don't happen according to schedule. There's certainly a bucketful of truth in the dictum, Timing is everything. If even just one item in your day's calendar is out of sync, the entire row of dominoes you've carefully set up is at risk.

Imagine the frustration the Israelites had as they wandered for nearly forty years in search of the Promised Land—a land that could have been reached in nine days, according to Deuteronomy 1:2. Keep in mind the promise part came from

God Himself. Many began to question God's promise. They even began to wonder if God had abandoned them.

You may feel the same way sometimes. Since you operate in a world ordered by time, you, too, probably have certain expectations of God's timing. When you ask God for an answer to prayer, you may hope for a quick response. When you look around and see the sorry state of the world around you, you may wonder what God's going to do about it—and when He's going to do it. When you consider the plight of the poor, the disenfranchised, the diseased, and the hungry, you may anxiously look for some sign that God has the solution to those plights scheduled on His calendar.

Yet God's timing is different from your timing. That's why it's important to learn how to wait on God. Waiting on God simply means allowing God to work things out according to His divine schedule.

Learning to wait on God reduces stress and puts life in perspective. Who doesn't know the stress of unmet deadlines? Not much fun. Learning to trust God's timing can help to reduce that anxiety.

Here's how. Begin with a little history lesson. Study examples of God's timing in the Bible. Look for ways He used time to affect the lives of His people. Read stories of God's uniquely timed intervention, beginning with the delivery of God's people from Egypt (Exodus 1—14). Look at how God used the many years in the wilderness to teach the Israelites about Himself (Numbers and Deuteronomy). You can also find evidence of God's unique sense of timing in New Testament stories. Look at the timing of God's appearance to Saul (Acts 9) and the sending of His spirit (Acts 2). Notice that in each situation, God showed up according to His schedule, and that in retrospect, that schedule made sense.

Next, understand that God can work outside of time as you know it. Keep in mind that God created time. What may seem like too long in a chronology based on seconds, minutes, and hours could be just right according to God's clock. Know that God is at work according to His schedule, even when the seconds tick away while you are awaiting an answer. God hears every prayer you offer and knows every question on your lips. But God's plan is too great to be contained in an earthly calendar.

You're also going to need a large portion of trust. God ultimately knows what's best for you and for the whole world. His timing in sending Jesus is a perfect example. And when Jesus comes again, that too will be at the perfect time. Believing this for the everyday requests and concerns you have requires that you trust that God really is in control.

The wise counsel of friends can come in handy as you learn to wait on God. A person outside of your immediate circumstance or question can usually offer a new perspective that sheds some light on the situation. Before you begin demanding that God bump your requests forward, talk with a friend. Broaden your view.

Finally, know that God still works in mysterious ways. All the previous explanations of God's timing could be trumped by something beyond earthly understanding. God reveals himself through the Bible, His Spirit, and through history—and yet full understanding of His timing may have to wait until heaven.

I Will

Trust that God is in control.   yes ____ no ____

Know that some questions I ask God won't have
immediate answers.   yes ____ no ____

Expect God to work things out according to His
timetable.   yes ____ no ____

Develop a patient spirit toward things I can't
control.   yes ____ no ____

Listen to friends' wisdom when frustrated by God's
timing.   yes ____ no ____

Accept that God works in mysterious ways.   yes ____ no ____

Things to Do

☐ *Study the first four chapters of Luke and consider the appropriateness of God's timing in sending Jesus.*

☐ *List personal prayer concerns you'd like God to answer.*

☐ *Ask God for an understanding of what it means to wait on God.*

☐ *Write a letter to God, expressing your biggest concerns about His response to world crises or tragedies.*

☐ *Read a book, perhaps Surprised by Joy, on the life of C. S. Lewis and his quest to understand God's mystery.*

☐ *Invite a friend to talk with you about his or her biggest "when will You answer?" questions for God.*

Things to Remember

God has set the members, each one of them, in the body just as He pleased.

1 CORINTHIANS 12:18 NKJV

If you are suffering according to God's will, keep on doing what is right and trust yourself to the God who made you, for he will never fail you.

1 PETER 4:19 TLB

O Lord, You are our Father. We are the clay and you are the Potter. We are all formed by your hand.
—Isaiah 64:8 TLB

Wait on the LORD; be of good courage, and He shall strengthen your heart; wait, I say, on the LORD!

PSALM 27:14 NKJV

The LORD said in Jacob's dream: "Behold, I am with you and will keep you wherever you go, and will bring you back to this land; for I will not leave you until I have done what I have spoken to you."

GENESIS 28:15 NKJV

God said to Moses, "I will take you as My people, and I will be your God. Then you shall know that I am the LORD your God who brings you out from under the burdens of the Egyptians."

EXODUS 6:7 NKJV

Those who know Your name will put their trust in You; for You, LORD, have not forsaken those who seek You.

PSALM 9:10 NKJV

Moses said to Israel, "The LORD your God . . . will not forsake you nor destroy you, nor forget the covenant of your fathers which He swore to them."

DEUTERONOMY 4:31 NKJV

True, some of them were unfaithful; but just because they broke their promises, does that mean God will break his promises?

ROMANS 3:3 NKJV

You have need of endurance, so that after you have done the will of God, you may receive the promise: "For yet a little while, and He who is coming will come and will not tarry."

HEBREWS 10:36–37 NKJV

Are we prepared to take the awful patient ways of God? We must not be infected by the world's valuation of either speed or success.

—JOHN B. PHILLIPS

The trouble is that I'm in a hurry, but God isn't.

—PHILLIPS BROOKS

God's Provision

What You Really Need

Jesus said, "Do not seek what you should eat or what you should drink, nor have an anxious mind. . . . Seek the kingdom of God, and all these things shall be added to you."

—Luke 12:29, 31 NKJV

The list of needs that people claim has been steadily rising over the past fifty years or so. A list that used to consist of little more than essentials such as food, water, clothing, and shelter has been expanded in recent time to include everything from specific kinds of food (no beets, please) to a computer and Internet hookup. In a world driven by the pursuit of more and more wants masquerading as needs, it's getting harder to sift through such a list and uncover the true necessities.

Go ahead and try. Pare back your own list until it's purely the needs. Once you've done this, however, Jesus has a surprising message for you: Stop pursuing items on this list too. Seek instead to grow your relationship with God.

Jesus' message is more than a challenge, however. It is a promise. Seek to know God and He'll take care of your needs and sustain you.

The key to trusting God for your needs begins with the understanding that Jesus' message is really all about priorities. An important step in this process is to be deliberate about your relationship with God. Don't assume that regular church attendance and Bible study are going to automatically make God a priority. Pray often. Invite God daily to reveal Himself to you. Ask God to direct your day—your decisions, the words you speak, even your thoughts. Enter each day anticipating new insight into God's will for your life.

Then be thankful. Make a quick mental list of what God has already provided in your life. Even if you consider your circumstances to be meager, your list is bound to be long. A thankful heart can help keep God at the top of your list.

Shrink your worry list. Examine areas in your life where anxiety rules. Does your worrying really make a positive difference in those situations? If not, dump the worry.

Finally, be diligent in whatever is your chosen profession. Trusting in God's provision doesn't mean quitting your job and sitting in a field with outstretched hands. God provides opportunities as well as the specific needs. Those opportunities may indeed be God's way of clothing you. Or of feeding you.

The closer you grow to God, the more you'll begin to see the many ways in which He provides—and the more you'll be willing to trust Him for that provision.

I Will

Order my priorities to focus on my relationship with
God first.   _yes_   _no_

Trust God to provide for my needs.   _yes_   _no_

Consider the real needs I have.   _yes_   _no_

Know that my needs are different than wants.   _yes_   _no_

Seek to grow closer to God every day.   _yes_   _no_

Be thankful for all God has already provided.   _yes_   _no_

Reduce the number of worries I currently have.   _yes_   _no_

Things to Do

☐ *Make a list of the actual needs you have.*

☐ *Ask God for the ability to trust in His provision.*

☐ *Read Jesus' Sermon on the Mount (Matthew 5—7) and consider the implications for how I approach wants and needs in life.*

☐ *Ask a pastor or other church leader for new ideas on how to seek God's kingdom.*

☐ *Write a thank-you note to God listing the ways in which He has provided for your needs.*

☐ *Surf the Internet for articles on a missionary (perhaps Jim Elliot or Hudson Taylor) and see what you can learn about trusting in God's provision.*

Things to Remember

We know that all things work together for good to those who love God, to those who are the called according to His purpose.

ROMANS 8:28 NKJV

Jesus said to them, "What kind of conversation is this that you have with one another as you walk and are sad?"

LUKE 24:17 NKJV

Though the fig tree may not blossom, nor fruit be on the vines; though the labor of the olive may fail, and the fields yield no food; though the flock may be cut off from the fold, and there be no herd in the stalls—yet I will rejoice in the LORD, I will joy in the God of my salvation.

HABAKKUK 3:17–18 NKJV

Humble yourselves under the mighty hand of God, that He may exalt you in due time.

1 PETER 5:6–7 NKJV

Commit everything you do to the LORD. Trust him, and he will help you.

PSALM 37:5 NLT

Disappointment, when it involves neither shame nor loss, is as good as success, for it supplies as many images to the mind, and as many topics to the tongue.

—SAMUEL JOHNSON

Why art thou disquieted; because it happeneth not to thee according to thy wishes and desires? Who is he that hath everything according to his will? Neither I, nor thou, nor any man upon the earth.

—THOMAS À KEMPIS

Pride

Before the Fall

Pride goes before destruction, and a haughty spirit before a fall.
—Proverbs 16:18 NKJV

There are two kinds of pride: good pride and bad pride. Good pride is a sense of satisfaction and joy for the accomplishments of others. It's the feeling you get when a child scores a last-second, winning touchdown or when a friend gets a well-deserved job promotion. Bad pride is self-focused. It's that wow-look-how-important-I-am boasting that demands the attention of others and dares them to consider their own worth in comparison with yours.

The Bible has a little to say about good pride, but a whole lot to say about bad pride. Reread the Scripture at the top of the page about pride and a haughty spirit. When it comes to bad pride, the Bible pulls no punches.

Isn't it okay to feel good about your accomplishments? Sure. It's not only okay, but it is also healthy to acknowledge your successes. You are a unique creation, and your gifts are likewise unique. There's no reason not to celebrate success. But bad pride enters the picture when you start to take credit for things you didn't really accomplish and when you put down the accomplishments of others in order for yours to look more important. The reason a fall is inevitable following bad pride is simple: You place yourself on a precarious pedestal when you exhibit bad pride. With every comment or action focused on making you seem more important than someone else, the rising platform on which you stand shrinks ever smaller.

Thankfully, avoiding bad pride is pretty easy. It begins by recognizing that your accomplishments are significant—but that they're no more significant than anyone else's. Instead of comparing your successes with others', simply enjoy them.

Give credit where credit is due. Did you really accomplish this task all by yourself? What role did others play? What role did God play? When you feel the rush of bad pride starting to take over, stop and look at the contributions of others. Ultimately, God gave you the abilities you employ, so He certainly ought to get some recognition for those great accomplishments.

See your accomplishments through another's eyes. Step back for a moment and imagine what another person might see when looking at your great works. Stepping into someone else's shoes can help bring a more balanced perspective and reduce the likelihood of bad pride.

Become other-focused instead of self-centered. Cheer the achievement of those around you. Revel in their accomplishments. If you practice good pride as often as possible, you'll soon find there's really no room left for bad pride.

I Will

Recognize that there are good and bad kinds of pride.

yes _____   _no_ _____

Evaluate my tendency to fall prey to bad pride.

yes _____   _no_ _____

Learn to give credit to those who assist in my successes.

yes _____   _no_ _____

Know that my accomplishments are important.

yes _____   _no_ _____

Attempt to see my accomplishments through the eyes of others.

yes _____   _no_ _____

Focus on the achievements of others instead of my own.

yes _____   _no_ _____

Things to Do

☐ _Thank God for the abilities and talents He's given you._

☐ _List an accomplishment you're proud of. Then determine if you've allowed bad pride to taint this accomplishment._

☐ _Invite a trusted friend to rate your inclination toward bad pride._

☐ _Read the book of Proverbs and find every mention of pride, then consider what each means to you._

☐ _Celebrate a recent success by a friend or family member._

☐ _Make yourself an AVOID BAD PRIDE reminder card and carry it with you in a wallet or purse or display it on a refrigerator._

☐ _Ask ten people for their definition of pride and see how many acknowledge the good and bad aspects of pride._

Things to Remember

A haughty look, a proud heart, and the plowing of the wicked are sin.

PROVERBS 21:4 NKJV

He who keeps instruction is in the way of life, but he who refuses correction goes astray.

PROVERBS 10:17 NKJV

Daniel said, "When [Nebuchadnezzar's] heart was lifted up, and his spirit was hardened in pride, he was deposed from his kingly throne, and they took his glory from him."

DANIEL 5:20 NKJV

The wicked in his proud countenance does not seek God; God is in none of his thoughts.

PSALM 10:4 NKJV

See that man who thinks he's so smart? You can expect far more from a fool than from him.

PROVERBS 26:12 THE MESSAGE

Therefore let him who thinks he stands take heed lest he fall.

1 CORINTHIANS 10:12 NKJV

Pride is the ground in which all other sins grow.

—WILLIAM BARKLEY

None are so empty as those who are full of themselves.

—BENJAMIN WHICHCOTE

Getting Along with Others

Woven Together

Behold, how good and how pleasant it is for brethren to dwell together in unity!

—*Psalm 133:1 NKJV*

If you were to put a dozen strangers in one room and ask them all to answer the same question—"What is the key to getting along with others?"—you'd doubtless get a dozen different answers. You might agree with some of their answers. Perhaps you'd disagree with a few. But no answer would likely capture word-for-word what you might choose say in response to the question.

Consider the people you spend time with each day. Do they think exactly the same way you do? Say the same things? Believe the same things? Of course not. The world is a stew that comprises uniquely crafted individuals. No one is exactly alike in appearance, action, or thought.

Perhaps that's why it can often be a trial to get along with others. In Bible times, communities were often defined by a common culture, rich with detailed traditions, rules, and regulations. But even in that more closed society, people didn't always get along. The psalmist may have been offering a gentle response to this very concern when he wrote about the pleasantness of unity.

In today's global society, the challenge to maintain unity is even greater. People with drastically different backgrounds, living situations, and life philosophies share space on the same block, in the same church, and around the same lunchroom. So how do you get along with others with whom you don't always agree?

Begin by accepting the fact that every person is a one-of-a-kind creation. Your opinions may differ greatly even if your cultural or social circumstances are similar.

Enter conversations with intent to learn or understand rather than determination to make your point. Careless words or reckless actions spawn most disunity. A little forethought and humility can prevent a casual conversation from spiraling into a battle of words.

Know what is nonnegotiable in your belief system before you interact with others. What values do you hold that you're not willing to compromise? What absolutes do you believe in? Be confident but not arrogant.

Unity requires patience too. Ask God for wisdom to know how you should respond and when.

Finally, be prepared to do what is necessary to mend ruptured relationships and to avoid grudges and bitterness. You're going to make mistakes—so are other people. Be prepared to act swiftly, to ask forgiveness, and to forgive in order to restore unity.

I Will

Pray for wisdom to know how to relate to others.
_____ yes _____ no

Accept that every person is unique.
_____ yes _____ no

Examine the way I usually interact with people who are different from me.
_____ yes _____ no

Enter conversations with a desire to understand.
_____ yes _____ no

Know what I believe before I dive into interactions with others.
_____ yes _____ no

Be patient when I'm with people who don't agree with me.
_____ yes _____ no

Forgive when someone's wronged me and ask for forgiveness when I mess up.
_____ yes _____ no

Things to Do

☐ *Ask God to give you more patience for the times you must interact with people you don't agree with.*

☐ *Make a list of the top three or four beliefs that are nonnegotiable when in conversation with others.*

☐ *Call a friend whom you may have hurt with your words or actions and ask for forgiveness.*

☐ *Invite a diverse group of friends over for an evening of food and conversation. Take the lead in helping others understand each other better.*

☐ *Draw an abstract picture of what disunity looks like, then draw another image depicting unity. Place these in a prominent place to remind you of the goal of unity.*

Things to Remember

Don't repay evil for evil. Don't snap back at those who say unkind things about you. Instead, pray for God's help for them, for we are to be kind to others, and God will bless us for it.

1 PETER 3:9 TLB

There is one body and one Spirit, just as you were called in one hope of your calling.

EPHESIANS 4:4 NKJV

If one part flourishes, every other part enters into the exuberance.

1 CORINTHIANS 12:25 THE MESSAGE

The multitude of those who believed were of one heart and one soul; neither did anyone say that any of the things he possessed was his own, but they had all things in common.

ACTS 4:32 NKJV

Let your conduct be worthy of the gospel of Christ, so that whether I come and see you or am absent, I may hear of your affairs, that you stand fast in one spirit, with one mind striving together for the faith of the gospel.

PHILIPPIANS 1:27 NKJV

If Christ is among us, then it is necessary that we sometimes yield up our own opinion for the sake of peace.

—THOMAS À KEMPIS

If there is any one secret of success, it lies in the ability to get the other person's point of view and see things from his angle as well as your own.

—HENRY FORD

Grace

When You Don't Get What You Deserve

It is God who saved us and chose us to live a holy life. He did this not because we deserved it, but because that was his plan long before the world began—to show his love and kindness to us through Christ Jesus.

—*2 Timothy 1:9* NKJV

One of the more enduring of the McDonald's commercial jingles made this rather bold pronouncement: "You deserve a break today." Did millions of Americans really deserve a break? Well, a busy life with no time to rest certainly sounds like a good reason to take a break. But, did the people really deserve a break? Though McDonald's may have used the concept of deservedness in a lighthearted way, it triggers the thought-provoking question, What do people really deserve?

If you examine the history of humanity as recorded in the Bible, there is no question about what people deserve. People messed up. By their own free will, they chose to disobey God and they ushered sin into the world. Because of sin, all of humanity deserves to be eternally separated from God. But God had a different idea. Through the gift of his son's life, He chose to save people from sin. He gave people the very thing they didn't deserve—the possibility of new life and an eternity by His side in heaven. This is the definition of grace.

The path to receiving grace is clearly marked in Scripture. When you choose to follow Christ and accept forgiveness, grace is yours. Instead of a Christ-less eternity, you are given eternal life. There is no cost—else it wouldn't be grace but something you had to work for.

Grace requires no further action on your part. You've been saved from destruction. But there are some natural responses to this grace that spring forth upon its acceptance. Will you lose your place in heaven if you don't respond in this way? No. And you won't lose it when you sin again—and you will. God's grace is big enough to handle your mistakes. Still, consider the following ways you might respond to this incredible gift from God.

Take advantage of every opportunity to become a fully devoted Christ-follower. If you don't already have a home church—seek one out that will challenge you to grow and encourage you along the way.

Pray often. Ask God for insight into His will for your life. Read the Bible to learn more about God and about what it means to follow God. Join a Bible study group and dig deeper into the Scriptures to find practical applications for your daily life.

Grace is free. Reflect on this gift that you don't deserve or take a backward glance at what you do deserve. Is there any more compelling reason to seek a closer relationship with God?

I Will

Thank God for the gift of grace.   _yes_   _no_

Consider how I should respond to God's grace.   _yes_   _no_

Seek to become a fully devoted Christ-follower.   _yes_   _no_

Examine my heart to see how I have responded to
God's gift of grace.   _yes_   _no_

Know that God's gift of grace can't be purchased
through good works.   _yes_   _no_

Be thankful that the gift of grace doesn't go away
when I sin.   _yes_   _no_

Things to Do

☐ Ask God to give you wisdom to know the right response to His gift of grace.

☐ Write a poem or song to God thanking Him for grace.

☐ Look up the word grace in a dictionary and compare the definition to your definition of God's grace.

☐ Find a copy of the Newsboys' song "Real Good Thing" and listen to it (it's on their Going Public CD).

☐ Ask a church friend or pastor to share their understanding of God's grace.

☐ Create a Because of Grace journal where you can list steps you take in response to God's grace. Write your first entries right away.

Things to Remember

If by grace, then it is no longer of works; otherwise grace is no longer grace. But if it is of works, it is no longer grace; otherwise work is no longer work.

ROMANS 11:6 NKJV

The law was given through Moses, but grace and truth came through Jesus Christ.

JOHN 1:17 NKJV

Prepare your minds for service and have self-control. All your hope should be for the gift of grace that will be yours when Jesus Christ is shown to you.

1 PETER 1:13 NCV

We believe that through the grace of the Lord Jesus Christ we shall be saved in the same manner as they.

ACTS 15:11 NKJV

God is able to make all grace abound toward you, that you, always having all sufficiency in all things, may have an abundance for every good work.

2 CORINTHIANS 9:8 NKJV

God gave that grace to us freely, in Christ, the One he loves.

EPHESIANS 1:6 NCV

Grace is not sought nor bought nor wrought. It is a free gift of Almighty God to needy mankind.

—BILLY GRAHAM

All men who live with any degree of serenity live by some assurance of grace.

—REINHOLD NIEBUHR

Swallowing Hard

Let every soul be subject to the governing authorities. For there is no authority except from God, and the authorities that exist are appointed by God.
—*Romans 13:1 NKJV*

One of the most difficult things to do in life is follow the instruction or leadership of someone you just don't get along with or respect. Whether this person is a supervisor at work, a parent at home, or a teacher at school, you find yourself cringing at the thought of having to carry out his or her directives.

More than likely, you've experienced this frustration yourself once or twice. Maybe you're experiencing it now. Do you ever get the urge to yell back at your supervisor? Or tell that teacher or parent what you really think about his leadership style? Maybe you have a few words for the local or national government leaders. Hold your tongue, at least until you understand the proper way to relate to people in authority with whom you don't get along.

Take a look first at those people in authority whom you do respect. How do you relate to these leaders? You gladly listen to their instruction. You move swiftly to fulfill their requests. Sometimes you go above and beyond their expectations. You do your best to earn their respect.

But that's easy. Acting the same way toward someone who believes in a completely different set of beliefs or values—now that can seem nearly impossible. You may be wondering if it's important to even try. Does it really matter? Is it that important to respect leaders you don't agree with?

The Bible says yes. In the book of Romans, Paul spoke directly to this issue, admonishing the Roman Christians to submit themselves to the governing authorities. Perhaps the Christians in Rome had been looking for Paul's blessing on their idea of offering allegiance only to Christ and rebellion toward Rome's pagan government. But Paul's response was clear, if a bit surprising: Show respect for all authority—even authority known for persecuting Christians—because all authority is ordained by God.

Tough as it may be to swallow, this truth is valid today. Of course that doesn't mean you have to agree with everyone in authority. It doesn't even mean you have to do everything that someone in authority asks you to (particularly things that would compromise your God-directed values). Respect, however, is required.

There are a few practical steps you can take to make this happen. To begin with, know that your situation is only temporary. Whether that temporary-ness is measured in weeks, months, or the rest of your life on earth, it still pales in comparison with the future life promised in heaven.

Demonstrate respect for the office or position the person holds. Whether or not you get along with the person in authority, you must respect their role. A teacher is responsible for passing along knowledge. A supervisor is responsible for the work of one or more employees. And parents are responsible for the upbringing of their children.

Be patient, quiet, and slow to react. A poor supervisor will make plenty of mistakes, but you don't have to react immediately and loudly to each one. Let the insignificant mistakes slide, and confront the important ones only after allowing time to consider a respectful way to approach your supervisor or the person in authority. You may be tempted to avoid all conflict, but a passive-aggressive approach isn't advised. Speak up about the things you disagree with. Just do so with a gentle spirit.

Learn everything you can. Some of the greatest life lessons come when people find themselves in situations that are less than optimal. You can discover a whole lot about how not to supervise someone by watching someone abuse or misuse his or her authority. You can also learn a lot about yourself— about your resilience, creativity, patience, and unconditional love. Gather as many life lessons as you can.

Be a peacemaker whenever possible. The pressures placed upon people in authority are often much greater than those put on those they lead, teach, or supervise. Don't add to their battles. Look for ways to bring peaceful solutions to your problems and to the problems of others. Encourage your leaders. Pray for them often.

Last, grow closer to God. Your relationship with God and your understanding of His word will help shape and guide your relationship with others who are in authority.

I Will

Know that God wants me to respect all authority on earth.

yes _____ *no* _____

Examine what it takes to show respect to authority figures I don't like or agree with.

yes _____ *no* _____

Understand that my current situation is only temporary.

yes _____ *no* _____

Demonstrate respect for the office of the person in authority.

yes _____ *no* _____

Practice patience when responding to things I don't agree with from a supervisor or someone in authority.

yes _____ *no* _____

Things to Do

☐ *Ask God to give you wisdom and patience for dealing with people in authority.*

☐ *Make a list of everyone who is an authority figure in your life (locally and nationally).*

☐ *Call someone in authority who is easy to respect and thank that person for being a good model of leadership.*

☐ *Write down three lessons you've learned about authority from a good leader and three you've learned from a not-so-good leader.*

☐ *Consider one problem area you have with someone in authority and brainstorm three ideas for dealing with that issue in a positive, respectful way.*

Things to Remember

Obey those who rule over you, and be submissive, for they watch out for your souls, as those who must give account. Let them do so with joy and not with grief, for that would be unprofitable for you.

HEBREWS 13:17 NKJV

Christians who are slaves should give their masters full respect so that the name of God and his teaching will not be shamed.

1 TIMOTHY 6:1 NLT

> *Do not exalt yourself in the presence of the king, and do not stand in the place of the great.*
> —Proverbs 25:6 NKJV

Those who have believing masters, let them not despise them because they are brethren, but rather serve them because those who are benefited are believers and beloved. Teach and exhort these things.

1 TIMOTHY 6:2 NKJV

The centurion said to Jesus, "I also am a man under authority, having soldiers under me. And I say to this one, 'Go,' and he goes; and to another, 'Come,' and he comes; and to my servant, 'Do this,' and he does it."

MATTHEW 8:9 NKJV

Let each of you look out not only for his own interests, but also for the interests of others.

PHILIPPIANS 2:4 NKJV

Whoever will not observe the law of your God and the law of the king, let judgment be executed speedily on him, whether it be death, or banishment, or confiscation of goods, or imprisonment.

EZRA 7:26 NKJV

Jeremiah wrote that the LORD said: Pray to the Lord for the city where you are living, because if good things happen in the city, good things will happen to you also.

JEREMIAH 29:7 NCV

Jesus answered and said to [the Pharisees and the Herodians], "Render to Caesar the things that are Caesar's, and to God the things that are God's." And they marveled at Him.

MARK 12:17 NKJV

If you're irresponsible to the state, then you're irresponsible with God, and God will hold you responsible.

ROMANS 13:2 THE MESSAGE

It is right to submit to higher authority whenever a command of God would not be violated.

—SAINT BASIL

Whatever makes them good Christians make them good citizens.

—DANIEL WEBSTER

Meet the Boss

Do your work with enthusiasm. Work as if you were serving the Lord, not as if you were serving only men and women.

—Ephesians 6:7 NCV

If you took a random survey of working people, you'd probably discover more than half the people don't really like their jobs. Many might even say that they despise their work. Perhaps that's why the idea of working for the weekend is so popular in American culture. People want to get away from the workplace as soon as possible.

Unfortunately, that kind of attitude can eat away at a person's ability to perform well on the job. An I-really-don't-want-to-be-here employee will often choose to do just enough work or give just enough effort to get by. Perhaps you've felt this way about your job from time to time too.

According to the Bible, however, just enough isn't good enough. Paul addressed this issue in a sweeping statement to the church at Colossae, where he encouraged the Christians there to do everything as if working for God.

Evaluate your current work habits. Do you show up to

work on time and work the expected number of hours? Do you use your time efficiently? Are you focused on the task at hand? Do you anticipate problems and attempt to avoid them whenever possible? If you're already doing these things, look for ways to do them even better.

Begin speaking positively about your job. If you already like your work, you've got this one nailed. But if you've been generally unhappy with your job, it's time to look for the positive points. A steady job of any kind is a good thing because, if nothing else, it helps to feed, clothe, and house you. What other good things can you say about your work? Brainstorm as big a list as possible. Then focus on those positives instead of on the negatives.

Consider the bigger purpose of your job. Does the company produce something that adds value to others' lives? So far as that product is compatible with your values, be passionate about it. Look beyond your piece of the work puzzle to the bigger picture. Look at your role as an employee. Your example of excellence can speak volumes to both your employer and your fellow employees. Perhaps one way you can make a difference is simply by being that example for others.

Working as if for God may seem like a daunting task, but it is extremely rewarding. Who knows, you could even be picked for a promotion because of your good work attitude. Just don't forget who your new boss is—God.

I Will

Consider what it means to work as if working for God. *yes*   *no*

Evaluate my current attitude toward work. *yes*   *no*

Focus on the positive aspects of my job. *yes*   *no*

Look for ways to be a good example at work. *yes*   *no*

Examine the bigger picture connected with my job and
how it has an impact on others. *yes*   *no*

Pursue excellence in all I do at work. *yes*   *no*

Learn to be happy with my work. *yes*   *no*

Things to Do

☐ *Create a reminder placard that says* GOD IS MY BOSS *or something similar and display it at home to remind you who you're really working for.*

☐ *Check out a book from the library on excellence. Compare book insights with your understanding of God's perspective on excellence.*

☐ *Talk with your supervisor and ask how you can improve as an employee.*

☐ *Make a list of the top ten good things about your job.*

☐ *Call a coworker and ask his or her opinion on your general attitude at work.*

☐ *Sign up for a class or find a specific resource that can improve your work skills.*

Things to Remember

Let your light so shine before men, that they may see your good works and glorify your Father in heaven.

MATTHEW 5:16 NKJV

Even while we were still there with you, we gave you this rule: "He who does not work shall not eat."

2 THESSALONIANS 3:10 TLB

Whatever you do in word or deed, do all in the name of the Lord Jesus, giving thanks to God the Father through Him.

COLOSSIANS 3:17 NKJV

Nehemiah sent messengers to them, saying, "I am doing a great work, so that I cannot come down. Why should the work cease while I leave it and go down to you?"

NEHEMIAH 6:3 NKJV

Six days you shall labor and do all your work.

EXODUS 20:9 NKJV

Make it your ambition to lead a quiet life, to mind your own business and to work with your hands.

1 THESSALONIANS 4:11 NIV

The best worship, however, is stout working.

—THOMAS CARLYLE

Hard work is a thrill and a joy when you are in the will of God.

—ROBERT A. COOK

Confidence

Bottled at the Source

God has not given us a spirit of fear, but of power and of love and of a sound mind.

—2 Timothy 1:7 NKJV

The starting point for a successful career in business, sports, education, and just about any other endeavor is often wrapped up in one character trait: confidence. Though skills and talents play a critical role in any success, self-confidence can mean the difference between a moderate success and an incredible one.

Most people desire self-confidence, but many don't know how to get it. One reason may be that the term *self-confidence* is somewhat of a misnomer. Though people may attempt to grow it on their own, confidence usually isn't self-generated at all. It comes from other sources such as parents, friends, coworkers, or even your environment. If your outside influences haven't provided you with a great sense of confidence, you may struggle to gain it.

No matter what your background or relational circumstances, you can find confidence from God. As Paul wrote in 2 Timothy, God didn't create you to be afraid or unsure in life, but to be filled with confidence, power, and love—exercising the gift of God in you.

Drawing confidence from your relationship with God starts when you recognize who God created you to be. First, you were created in God's image. That ought to provide some confidence, knowing that you share some of the qualities of God Himself. But if that's a difficult concept for you to get a handle on (and it is a bit overwhelming), you can find confidence in the truth that God created you—and called that creation good. Knowing that God loves you for who you are can propel you forward in life with a sense of confidence that outlasts even the encouragement of others.

Another key to gaining confidence is simply to understand what it is—and what it isn't. Some people mistake boldness or aggressive behavior for confidence. Real confidence is knowing that your motives are good, your chosen path is true, and your abilities are sufficient for the task. Braggadocio is not usually a sign of confidence, but an attempt to bolster its lack.

Confidence also grows when you realize that your source of confidence, God, has provided His Spirit to guide and direct you along your life trek. You are not alone in life. God goes with you. This is especially important to grasp when you're facing a trial or challenge.

When others offer encouragement, go ahead and let that build your confidence. You're receiving a wonderful gift. But when the kind words of others seem absent, drink from the unending source of confidence: your relationship with God.

I Will

Know that the greatest source for confidence is a
relationship with God.   *yes*   *no*

Enjoy the self-confidence that comes from knowing
I'm created in God's image.   *yes*   *no*

Feel good about myself because God loves me for
who I am.   *yes*   *no*

Count on God's Spirit to help me maintain
confidence in life's challenging times.   *yes*   *no*

Understand that confidence is important to life
success.   *yes*   *no*

Recognize that boldness and aggressive behavior
aren't the same thing as confidence.   *yes*   *no*

Things to Do

☐ *Think back on a time when you struggled with confidence. Thank God for the confidence He's given you and for the confidence He will give you in the future.*

☐ *Watch a popular TV drama and compare how Hollywood depicts self-confidence to what you know about confidence that's anchored in a relationship with God.*

☐ *List five reasons you ought to feel confident in life.*

☐ *List five obstacles to self-confidence you face today (or have faced in the past).*

☐ *Invite a friend you see as confident to share what gives him or her that confidence.*

Things to Remember

I am sure that God, who began the good work within you, will continue his work until it is finally finished on that day when Christ Jesus comes back again.

PHILIPPIANS 1:6 NLT

Therefore take heart, men, for I believe God that it will be just as it was told me.

ACTS 27:25 NKJV

Then David said to the Philistine, "You come to me with a sword, with a spear, and with a javelin. But I come to you in the name of the LORD of hosts, the God of the armies of Israel, whom you have defied."

1 SAMUEL 17:45 NKJV

Beloved, if our heart does not condemn us, we have confidence toward God.

1 JOHN 3:21 NKJV

We are always confident, knowing that while we are at home in the body we are absent from the Lord.

2 CORINTHIANS 5:6 NKJV

Do not cast away your confidence, which has great reward.

HEBREWS 10:35 NKJV

Our confidence in Christ does not make us lazy, negligent, or careless, but on the contrary it awakens us, urges us on, and makes us active in living righteous lives and doing good. There is no self-confidence to compare with this.

—ULRICH ZWINGLI

In sorrow and suffering, go straight to God with confidence, and you will be strengthened, enlightened and instructed.

—SAINT JOHN OF THE CROSS

Kindness

Fruit to Share

The fruit of the Spirit is love, joy, peace, longsuffering, kindness, goodness, faithfulness, gentleness, self-control. Against such there is no law.

—Galatians 5:22–23 NKJV

Two distinctly different kinds of experiences stand out when people reflect on their past and current relationships: acts of malice and acts of kindness. It's no surprise that unkind acts come to the surface when people think about their relationships: Pain has a long memory. Acts of kindness stand out for a different reason: They are rare and wonderful. While acts of malice really have more to do with the person who is causing the pain, acts of kindness focus directly and unselfishly on the person receiving the kindness. True kindness is all about doing something for someone else without expectation of getting something in return.

Take a moment to reflect on the kindness that's been shown to you over the years. How do you feel when you think about the kind things others have done for you? You most likely feel loved. That's what kindness is all about—love. Kindness is born out of a love for others and is prompted by a love for God.

The power and positive influence of kindness is beyond

measure. It can heal wounds visible and invisible. It can build bridges. It can comfort, encourage, and challenge others to grow.

Since kindness starts with love, the first thing you must do if you want to show kindness is to love people. Loving others begins with loving God. As Paul noted in his description of the fruit of the spirit, love, kindness, and all the fruits of the spirit are the natural result of a love for God and a growing relationship with Him. The more you get to know God, the more you learn to love people.

While it may be more convenient and comfortable to show kindness to people you know, it is just as important to show kindness to strangers. In fact, showing kindness to strangers may be the most fulfilling of all good deeds. Whenever someone is truly surprised by kindness, that person's joy and sense of being loved is multiplied—as is the giver's.

Helping to meet needs is probably the most visible and familiar way to show kindness. To do this, you must first know the person's needs. That's easy if the person is a close friend or family member, and a bit more challenging if the person is a casual acquaintance or a stranger. Still, there are ways to uncover a person's needs: Talk with someone who knows the person, observe the person's life situation, or simply ask the person how you can help. Needs may not always be obvious. An unmowed lawn may be evidence of a simple, visible need (the need for a lawn mower that works, for example) or it could hide a deeper need (the need for a friend or someone who can help that person work through a downtime or depression).

Kindness is also an attitude. If you've ever worked in a retail establishment with a focus on customer service, you've probably already heard a dozen speeches on the power of a smile. That speech, no matter how many times you've heard it, still holds true. One smile to a stranger could make a dreary day suddenly bright. When you do life in an optimistic way, kind words and deeds flow naturally to the people around you. While it may not be possible for you to always carry a positive attitude, make it your goal to live life with as much positivity as you can. You'll even have a beneficial impact on people you never meet.

Going above and beyond someone's expectations is one of the most powerful ways to show kindness. Jesus taught the importance of this do-more-than-someone-asks approach to life when he described the proper way to respond to someone who asks you to carry something one mile—he said, carry it two miles. Going the extra mile today might mean washing your friend's truck after you borrow it instead of just filling it with gas; shoveling a neighbor's driveway in addition to the sidewalk you already offered to clear; or following up a get-well card with a phone call and visit to see what you can do to help.

Kindness is contagious. Your goodness toward one person will often prompt that person to do something kind for someone else. Sow kindness and the whole world will reap its benefits.

I Will

Seek to love God more so I can lean how to love other people more.

yes   no

Know that kindness comes out of a love for others.

yes   no

Reflect on the kindness shown to me and be thankful for it.

yes   no

Look for ways to develop a positive, kind attitude.

yes   no

Go the extra mile when I relate to others.

yes   no

Help meet others' needs whenever possible.

yes   no

Things to Do

☐ *Compare what you know about the biblical concept of kindness with the typical example of relationships as shown on a popular TV sitcom.*

☐ *Study all of the fruits of the spirit in Galatians 5:22–23 and score yourself on how well you exhibit each one.*

☐ *Determine one kind thing you can do for a family member this week.*

☐ *List three ways people have shown you kindness in the past week.*

☐ *Invite a friend to lunch and discuss what impact a full-time kind attitude might have on your work relationships.*

☐ *Think back on the events in a recent day and determine ways you could have added kindness to your activities.*

☐ *Buy a favorite snack food for a friend and deliver it to that person secretly.*

Things to Remember

She opens her mouth with wisdom, and on her tongue is the law of kindness.

PROVERBS 31:26 NKJV

"The mountains shall depart and the hills be removed, but My kindness shall not depart from you, nor shall My covenant of peace be removed," says the Lord, who has mercy on you.

ISAIAH 54:10 NKJV

> Jesus said, "If you lend to those from whom you hope to receive back, what credit is that to you? For even sinners lend to sinners to receive as much back."
> —Luke 6:34 NKJV

The natives showed us unusual kindness; for they kindled a fire and made us all welcome, because of the rain that was falling and because of the cold.

ACTS 28:2 NKJV

The stranger who dwells among you shall be to you as one born among you, and you shall love him as yourself; for you were strangers in the land of Egypt: I am the LORD your God.

LEVITICUS 19:4 NKJV

"With a little wrath I hid My face from you for a moment; but with everlasting kindness I will have mercy on you," says the LORD, your Redeemer.

ISAIAH 54:8 NKJV

If you see your neighbor's ox or sheep wandering away, don't pretend not to see it. Take it back to its owner.

DEUTERONOMY 22:21 NKJV

Each of us should please his neighbor for his good, to build him up.

ROMANS 15:2 NIV

What is desired in a man is kindness, and a poor man is better than a liar.

PROVERBS 19:22 NKJV

Thus says the LORD of hosts: "Execute true justice, show mercy and compassion everyone to his brother."

ZECHARIAH 7:9 NKJV

When we have the opportunity to help anyone, we should do it. But we should give special attention to those who are in the family of believers.

GALATIANS 6:10 NCV

Kindness: Love in Action.
—CHARLES ALLEN

He who sows courtesy reaps friendship, and he who plants kindness gathers love.
—SAINT BASIL

Sharing Your Faith

There's Still Work to Do

He said to them, "Go into all the world and preach the gospel to every creature."

—*Mark 16:15* NKJV

The last thing Jesus said before he ascended into heaven was, "Go and make disciples of all the nations." Now there's a daunting task. Can you imagine the expressions on the faces of Jesus' friends as they heard his command? You can bet more that a few jaws dropped. Perhaps someone even thought, Go and make disciples of the nations? Yeah right. Me and what army?

Of course that was a couple millennia ago. A quick survey of the nations today will come up with approximately two billion people who categorize themselves as Christians. Not bad, considering that Jesus' initial missionary group consisted of about a dozen people. Keep in mind, though, that the world population is somewhere around six billion—so there's still work to do, about four billion!

This idea of making disciples is often referred to as "sharing your faith" or "evangelizing." However, these phrases often send a chill down the spine of even the most dedicated Christians. Why? Because for some people, they paint a mental picture of a rather imposing street preacher thumping a huge

Bible on a street corner and calling out, "If you don't love Jesus, you're going to hell!" to passersby.

Thankfully, God doesn't ask everyone to be a street-corner preacher. Many are called to a different kind of evangelism—something commonly referred to as relationship evangelism, which is sharing about God's love to someone you know, someone who trusts you.

If you walk up to a stranger and say "God loves you," that stranger may listen to you, but just as likely may walk away shaking his head or laughing. But if the topic of God's love flows into a talk with a friend, that friend is probably going to listen with as much interest as in any other conversation.

Before you attempt to share your faith relationally, however, it's important to know what you believe—and know which beliefs are essential for a relationship with God. Focusing on such potentially divisive topics as the end times, worship style, or even baptism can confuse and misguide rather than bring someone closer to God.

The first step is straightforward: Develop relationships. Whether you're at the office, at the gym, or sharing a table at a restaurant, you can begin to build relationships with others. Get to know the other person. Learn about his or her interests, share a cup of coffee and a laugh. You may find out the person is already a Christian. Or you may discover the person knows little or nothing at all about faith. Either way, as you grow in your relationship, you'll build trust.

Here's a quick note about trust. You may feel that you ought to hide your faith early in the relationship so you don't scare your new friend. Don't. That doesn't mean you should wave your beliefs around like a flag. Just be yourself. If something comes up in conversation that would naturally prompt you to talk about your relationship with God, go ahead and do so. Being true to your beliefs is an important component in building trust, and it also says something about how you value your relationship with Christ.

Pray daily. Ask God to soften the hearts of those people with whom you desire to share your faith. Ask God for wisdom in knowing what to say it.

Be patient. You'll discover that some nonbelievers you build relationships with are hungry for more information about God's love, and a few will even be excited about what you have to share and wonder why you didn't tell them sooner. Others will feel uncomfortable and may even end the relationship because of their discomfort. Still others—and this may be the majority—will maintain the relationship, accepting you for who you are, but continuing to say "that God stuff just isn't for me." You may never see a change in that person's heart—or you may get a letter twenty years from now saying, "Hey, I finally get it! I've chosen to follow Christ!" Your job is simply to love people and tell them about God's love—sealing of the deal is between that person and God.

In your hearts set apart Christ as Lord. Always be prepared to give an answer to everyone who asks you to give the reason for the hope that you have. But do this with gentleness and respect.
—1 Peter 3:15 NIV

I Will

Know that Jesus wants me to share my faith.   _yes_   _no_

Realize that I may not be called to share faith with
a bold, in-your-face style.   _yes_   _no_

Learn what it means to share faith through
relationships.   _yes_   _no_

Seek out relationships with people I don't know and
who may be nonbelievers.   _yes_   _no_

Pray for confidence to reach out to those who don't
know Christ.   _yes_   _no_

Christ is ultimately between the person and God.   _yes_   _no_

Things to Do

☐ *Ask God for wisdom in knowing how you ought to relate to people who are nonbelievers.*

☐ *Make a list of five people you know who aren't yet Christians. Put your list in a wallet or purse as a reminder to pray for them often.*

☐ *Read one or more books on how to share your faith with others.*

☐ *Ask a pastor or other church leader how to lead someone to Christ.*

☐ *Write out the beliefs you see as essential in a relationship with God and then list those that aren't deal-breakers for your faith.*

☐ *Identify one person who may be a nonbeliever you would like to develop a relationship with. Call that person and invite him or her to lunch or some other nonthreatening activity.*

Things to Remember

Jesus said, "You are the light of the world. A city that is set on a hill cannot be hidden."

MATTHEW 5:14 NKJV

Daily in the temple, and in every house, they did not cease teaching and preaching Jesus as the Christ.

ACTS 5:42 NKJV

Jesus said, "No one can come to Me unless the Father who sent Me draws him; and I will raise him up at the last day."

JOHN 6:44 NKJV

Go therefore and make disciples of all the nations, baptizing them in the name of the Father and of the Son and of the Holy Spirit.
—Matthew 28:19 NKJV

We are ambassadors for Christ, as though God were pleading through us: we implore you on Christ's behalf, be reconciled to God.

2 CORINTHIANS 5:20 NKJV

Jesus said, "When the Holy Spirit has come upon you, you will receive power to testify about me with great effect, to the people in Jerusalem, throughout Judea, in Samaria, and to the ends of the earth, about my death and resurrection."

ACTS 1:8 TLB

The Good News about the Kingdom will be preached throughout the whole world, so that all nations will hear it.

MATTHEW 24:14 NLT

Paul wrote: I make known to you, brethren, that the gospel which was preached by me is not according to man. For I neither received it from man, nor was I taught it, but it came through the revelation of Jesus Christ.

GALATIANS 1:11–12 NKJV

You be watchful in all things, endure afflictions, do the work of an evangelist, fulfill your ministry.

2 TIMOTHY 4:5 NKJV

He that goeth forth and weepeth, bearing precious seed, shall doubtless come again with rejoicing, bringing his sheaves with him.

PSALM 126:6 KJV

To me, who am less than the least of all the saints, this grace was given, that I should preach among the Gentiles the unsearchable riches of Christ.

EPHESIANS 3:8 NKJV

The way from God to a human heart is through a human heart.

—SAMUEL GORDON

I cared not where or how I lived, or what hardships I went through, so that I could but gain souls for Christ. While I was asleep, I dreamed of these things, and when I awoke, the first thing I thought of was this great work.

—DAVID BRAINERD

Giving to God

Reach into Your Wallet and Smile

Let each one give as he purposes in his heart, not grudgingly or of necessity; for God loves a cheerful giver.

—*2 Corinthians 9:7 NKJV*

Few pastors really enjoy talking about money on a Sunday morning. It's no wonder. The area of personal finances is a touchy subject for just about anyone who's ever held a dollar bill. Still, most pastors take a couple weeks out of each year to speak about stewardship, tithing, or giving.

Too often, people stop listening the moment a pastor begins to talk about money. They hear the pastor say something about giving ten percent and immediately grab their wallet or purse and hold tight to their cash. But when they tune out too early, they miss the real point: Giving is a spiritual issue, not a monetary one. God doesn't need your money, but He desires your love and obedience. When Paul said that God loves a "cheerful giver," he was saying that God is most interested in the heart, not the size of the check.

The key to learning how to be a cheerful giver begins with acknowledgment that God is the owner of all the stuff you have. You, on the other hand, are the caretaker of God's treasure. Getting your heart around this truth can be a real test, especially since the world at large preaches loudly and often that you are only as significant as the stuff you own. If you feel a compulsion to give that's born out of guilt or a sense of duty, your heart may not be ready. Do you give because of your love for God? Your concern for others? When your heart is right, giving is easy.

Check your priorities. God desires your best in all areas of life. When it comes to giving, that means setting aside your portion for God before you calculate the rest of your budget needs. If you wait until everything else is paid off before setting aside something for God, there usually isn't much left.

Finally, trust God's promise. The only example in Scripture where God challenges you to test Him is in this area of giving. God says—go ahead and give and just see what I give you back in return. Does that mean you're going to win the lotto or get a big promotion if you give big? No. And the idea of receiving something from God shouldn't be your motivation for giving either. But this much is true: You can't out-give God. Learn to trust in God's promise, and giving can become a wonderful faith adventure.

I Will

Realize that God desires the first and best of what I
earn or own.

yes _____ *no* _____

Know that God challenges me to test Him in this
area of giving.

yes _____ *no* _____

Look forward to the faith adventure that comes with
learning how to be giving.

yes _____ *no* _____

Know that giving isn't a monetary issue, but a
spiritual one.

yes _____ *no* _____

Understand that churches need donations in order to
survive and thrive.

yes _____ *no* _____

Examine my attitude toward giving.

yes _____ *no* _____

Things to Do

☐ *Ask God to give you a heart for giving.*

☐ *Review your budget and consider what it would take to give to God off
the top.*

☐ *Read the story of the widow's mite in Luke 21:1–4 and examine what
that story implies about how you ought to give.*

☐ *Invite a Christian friend to discuss what it means to be a caretaker of
your belongings rather than an owner.*

☐ *List five ways you can give back to God in addition to monetary giving.*

☐ *Choose one thing you can do without and determine to give the money
to God instead.*

Things to Remember

Jesus said, "When you do a charitable deed, do not let your left hand know what your right hand is doing, that your charitable deed may be in secret; and your Father who sees in secret will Himself reward you openly."

MATTHEW 6:3–4 NKJV

"Bring all the tithes into the storehouse, that there may be food in My house, and try Me now in this," says the LORD of hosts, "If I will not open for you the windows of heaven and pour out for you such blessing that there will not be room enough to receive it."

MALACHI 3:10 NKJV

King David said, "I have already given this for the Temple, but now I am also giving my own treasures of gold and silver, because I really want the Temple of my God to be built."

1 CHRONICLES 29:3 NCV

If there is among you a poor man of your brethren, within any of the gates in your land which the LORD your God is giving you, you shall not harden your heart nor shut your hand from your poor brother.

DEUTERONOMY 15:7 NKJV

The basic question is not how much of our money we should give to God, but how much of God's money we should keep for ourselves.

—J. OSWALD SANDERS

There is a blessed kind of giving, which, though it makes the purse lighter, makes the crown heavier.

—THOMAS WATSON

Complaining

Keep It to Yourself

Do all things without complaining and disputing.

—Philippians 2:14 NKJV

Imagine what it would be like to have a full-time complainer follow you around for a day. You'd soon discover that your house is too small, your job is no fun, you have bad taste in restaurants, and your clothes don't match . . . that is, if you survived the day without going crazy. Complainers can suck the life out of just about any circumstance. At work, a complainer can make a fun job into a chore. At home, a complainer can turn a place of rest into a place of stress.

Can you picture someone in your world who plays this role? Perhaps that person is you. Or maybe you're just a part-time complainer. Paul had a clear message for all who complain or have a negative attitude: Don't. In his letter to the Philippian church, Paul encouraged the Christians there to do all things without complaining. It's likely that Paul's words sounded a lot easier to obey than they actually were. But there are ways to avoid being a complainer.

Always look on the bright side of life. Okay, that may sound a bit trite. But there is a real power in looking at what's working right in any given situation. If you search for something that's wrong or negative in your circumstance, you can almost always find something to complain about. That's the reality of an imperfect life in an imperfect world. But what if you redirect that search and look for something that's good about the situation? You will probably find something to be thankful for. At the end of the day, a collection of positive experiences or thoughts is going to go a long way toward making your life fun, fulfilling, and enjoyable.

Realize that most complaints do little to improve a situation. Instead of complaining, look for positive, practical solutions to the problem. A complaint about a work procedure may seem like a step in the right direction, but it goes nowhere fast if you don't follow through with helping to find a solution. Rather than count on complaining to change things, offer suggestions.

Complaints are like roadblocks. And each complaint on the path from point A to point B increases the length of your trip. That doesn't mean you shouldn't address improprieties or unfairness. Both ought to be identified and dealt with appropriately—but with positive actions, not just grumbles about how things are so horrible.

I Will

Take action to solve a problem instead of to complain about it.　　yes　　no

Know that life isn't always going to be fair.　　yes　　no

Address unfairness and other issues directly, rather than simply complain about them.　　yes　　no

Evaluate my tendency to complain.　　yes　　no

Know that it's best not to be a complainer.　　yes　　no

Understand that complaining doesn't often solve a problem.　　yes　　no

Look for the positive in any given situation.　　yes　　no

Things to Do

☐ Ask God for wisdom to avoid complaining and be more focused on the positive.

☐ List five complaints you've had in the past week.

☐ Ask a close friend to rate your tendency to be a complainer.

☐ Think back on a recent complaint you had and come up with three positives you could have considered instead or one action you could have taken to solve the situation.

☐ Have a few friends join you in choosing the television character who is the greatest complainer.

☐ Talk with a pastor or other church leader about areas in your life where you tend to complain inappropriately.

Things to Remember

Do not say, "Why were the former days better than these?" For you do not inquire wisely concerning this.

ECCLESIASTES 7:10 NKJV

Both bad and good things come by the command of the Most High God.

LAMENTATIONS 3:38 NCV

Martha was distracted with much serving, and she approached Him and said, "Lord, do You not care that my sister has left me to serve alone? Therefore tell her to help me."

LUKE 10:40 NKJV

I am always content with what happens for I know that what God chooses is better than what I choose.

—EPICTETUS

Friends, don't complain about each other. A far greater complaint could be lodged against you, you know. The Judge is standing just around the corner.

JAMES 5:9 THE MESSAGE

Don't say all you'd like to say lest you hear something you wouldn't like to hear.

—SEAMUS MACMANUS

These are grumblers, complainers, walking according to their own lusts; and they mouth great swelling words, flattering people to gain advantage.

JUDE 16 NKJV

The people complained against Moses, saying, "What shall we drink?" So he cried out to the LORD, and the LORD showed him a tree. When he cast it into the waters, the waters were made sweet.

EXODUS 15:24–25 NKJV

Resetting Time

In its place you have clothed yourselves with a brand-new nature that is continually being renewed as you learn more and more about Christ, who created this new nature within you.

—*Colossians 3:10* NKJV

Looking backward can be painful. Memories of poorly chosen paths bring with them jarringly potent echoes of the original accompanying ache. Reflecting on a history scattered with wounds, mistakes, and agonizing experiences can also stifle forward progress, but it doesn't have to. No one can fully escape the past, but a decision to follow Christ offers a new start, a prospect that promises to eclipse even the most unpleasant narrative.

Your new start begins with forgiveness. When you ask God to forgive your sins, He resets your internal life-experience clock. Then you can begin to discover your new nature. Old habits die hard, but a life lived in pursuit of God's will can turn harmful habits into distant memories. No longer are you locked into bad patterns that may have defined your experience. In their place are new opportunities—opportunities to learn God-directed ways to be in relationship with others, to be a faithful follower, and to understand who you really are in Christ.

As you take each step in the new journey that beings with a fresh start, look for God's guidance along the way. The past has a way of sneaking up on you, but with God's Spirit to guide you, you can dodge those tugs toward old behaviors. Pray for strength to move forward. Examine the Scriptures for good advice, wisdom, and insight-filled stories on what it means to have new life in Christ.

Change your environment. Throw away reminders of past mistakes. Stop going to old haunts if they tempt you to return to your old nature. And consider avoiding relationships that encourage looking backward. Instead, develop new relationships that can help you see the future.

Know that God still loves you when you make mistakes. A new start doesn't mean a perfect life, but it does mean you can finally leave the past behind you. There is no longer any need to revisit the mistakes you've made; they've been forgiven. Life will continue to have its uncomfortable moments—errors of judgment, wrongly chosen paths, misspoken words—but the Reset button that comes with your relationship with Christ will always be waiting for you to press.

Hang on to hope. More than anything else, the promise of a new start is the promise of hope. Hope is renewed when you come to God. Your future becomes bright. The past dims. There is nothing to stop you from living a full and fulfilling life.

I Will

Understand that a new start in Christ begins with forgiveness.

<u>yes</u>   <u>no</u>

Know that looking backward can be stifling and painful.

<u>yes</u>   <u>no</u>

Examine what it means to have a new nature in Christ.

<u>yes</u>   <u>no</u>

Trust God's guidance as I move forward in life.

<u>yes</u>   <u>no</u>

Count on God's love even when I mess up.

<u>yes</u>   <u>no</u>

Discover hope when I ask God for a fresh start.

<u>yes</u>   <u>no</u>

Things to Do

☐ Ask God to give you the confidence to move ahead and the ability to stop bad habits.

☐ Make yourself a visual reminder that God offers a new start. Display this reminder in your home or car.

☐ Go through old papers, books, and memorabilia and throw away things that remind you of your former ways.

☐ List past experiences that you'd like to erase with a new start.

☐ Search the Internet or library for information about a rebel who made a fresh start after becoming a Christian, such as Nicky Cruz.

☐ Study the book of Romans to better understand what it means to live with a new life in Christ.

Things to Remember

If anyone is in Christ, he is a new creation; old things have passed away; behold, all things have become new.

2 CORINTHIANS 5:17 NKJV

We were therefore buried with him through baptism into death in order that, just as Christ was raised from the dead through the glory of the Father, we too may live a new life.

ROMANS 6:4 NIV

If you return to the Almighty, you will be built up; you will remove iniquity far from your tents.

JOB 22:23 NKJV

The LORD said, "I will give you a new heart and put a new spirit within you; I will take the heart of stone out of your flesh and give you a heart of flesh."

EZEKIEL 36:26 NKJV

We have been delivered from the law, having died to what we were held by, so that we should serve in the newness of the Spirit and not in the oldness of the letter.

ROMANS 7:6 NKJV

A thousand years of remorse over a wrong act would not please God as much as a change of conduct and a reformed life.

—A. W. TOZER

Sleep with clean hands, either kept clean all day by integrity or washed clean at night by repentance.

—JOHN DONNE

Working on the "Forget"

Be gentle and ready to forgive; never hold grudges. Remember, the Lord forgave you, so you must forgive others.

—*Colossians 3:13* TLB

I forgive you.

Those three words are often difficult to utter, and they sometimes seem downright impossible to abide by. Consider the times you've been wronged in recent months. Perhaps someone lied to you. Maybe someone said unkind things about you. What feelings do you have when you think back to those circumstances? Anger? Frustration? Disappointment? Notice how easy it is to recapture some of the bitterness?

When someone causes you pain, it's not always easy to forgive. It's so much easier to hold a grudge, to silently keep punishing the person for his or her wrongs. In a twisted sort of way, holding back forgiveness seems to even the score.

The Bible, however, teaches a different message about forgiveness. In no uncertain terms, it says to "forgive others just as Christ forgave you."

When Paul wrote members of the Colossian church, he was responding to false teachings that had infected their beliefs. Much of Paul's letter was written to refute this heresy and to help the Colossian church members find their way back to living according to Jesus' teachings. It's significant for two reasons that Paul talked about forgiveness in his letter. First, Paul knew that the confusion brought about by heretical teachings and the subsequent rediscovery of the truth could lead to bitterness and hurt among the members. Second, the message of forgiveness would point them back to the focal point of true faith: that Jesus died to forgive their sins.

This focal point of faith is the greatest motivation for deciding to forgive others. Since Jesus paid the ultimate price for your forgiveness, what right do you have to deny forgiveness to those who wrong you? Jesus said it even more directly: "If you forgive others, God will forgive you."

Forgiveness, like so many other actions of faith, begins with a change of heart. Sometimes you need to forgive directly. You need to stand up and say to another person, "I forgive you." This is important especially if the person who has wronged you has asked for forgiveness. Offering forgiveness helps to mend that person's pain as well as your own bitterness.

There are also times you need to forgive without words. Maybe the person who wronged you has moved away or is no longer living. You still need to forgive that person in your heart. Forgiveness opens the door to personal healing and removes the tentacles that threaten to pull you back into anger or resentment.

You'll need to forgive often. When the disciple Peter asked Jesus how many times he was to forgive someone, Peter probably thought he was being generous by suggesting "seven." Imagine his surprise when Jesus said, "seventy times seven." Rather than an actual number (though 490 is a lot), Jesus' answer implied there was no limit to forgiveness. You'll probably experience moments when you don't think you have any forgiveness left. Pray for patience in those times. Step away from the situation and recall Jesus' command to "keep on forgiving." Then, when you're ready, forgive again.

Not everyone who wrongs you does so with intent to harm. When Jesus was on the cross, he said about the very people who unwittingly sent him to die: "Forgive them, for they don't know what they're doing." Perhaps the person who damaged you didn't intend to. Members of the human race are notorious for their ability to say or do things without thinking them through first. Forgive those who make such errors. Perhaps they were just careless or merely clueless.

Now comes the hardest part: the forgetting. When we ask God for forgiveness, He not only forgives, but He also removes those sins as far as the east is from the west. He forgets them. You may think you have forgiveness down just fine, until someone or something comes along to remind you of the past. Then you remember the hurt and bitter taste creeps into your mouth. Once you've forgiven someone, stop dwelling on the situation. Give the person the benefit of the doubt that things will be better. It may take some time to get beyond the hurt. That's okay. But as soon as you can, start looking ahead. Let the memory of the pain fade away as you walk step by step into the future.

I Will

Learn to forgive others just as Christ forgave me. _yes_ _no_

Acknowledge that it can be difficult to forgive others. _yes_ _no_

Know that it is right to offer forgiveness. _yes_ _no_

Understand that sometimes I need to forgive people directly. _yes_ _no_

Forgive those who may have hurt me but no longer are around to talk to. _yes_ _no_

Forgive without limits. _yes_ _no_

Endeavor to forget after I've forgiven someone. _yes_ _no_

Things to Do

☐ *Thank God for forgiving your sins and ask Him for strength to forgive others.*

☐ *Talk with a friend about a grudge you've been holding against someone and ask for advice on how to get rid of that grudge.*

☐ *Think about someone you haven't forgiven but should. Call that person or write a letter, offering your forgiveness.*

☐ *List three things that make it difficult to forgive, and five reasons it's right to forgive.*

☐ *On a piece of paper, list something you've forgiven but are having a hard time forgetting. Then tear up that paper or burn it in a fireplace to symbolize your desire to forget.*

Things to Remember

Peter came to Him and said, "Lord, how often shall my brother sin against me, and I forgive him? Up to seven times?" Jesus said to him, "I do not say to you, up to seven times, but up to seventy times seven."

MATTHEW 18:21–22 NKJV

Jesus said, "Take heed to yourselves. If your brother sins against you, rebuke him; and if he repents, forgive him."

LUKE 17:3 NKJV

Be kind and merciful, and forgive others, just as God forgave you because of Christ.
—Ephesians 4:32 CEV

Jesus said, "If you forgive others for their sins, your Father in heaven will also forgive you for your sins."

MATTHEW 6:14 NCV

Then Jesus said, "Father, forgive them, for they do not know what they do."

LUKE 23:34 NKJV

Jesus said, "I assure you that any sin can be forgiven."

MARK 3:28 NLT

As they stoned him, Stephen prayed, "Lord Jesus, receive my spirit." And he fell to his knees, shouting, "Lord, don't charge them with this sin!" And with that, he died.

ACTS 7:59–60 NLT

Bless those who persecute you; bless and do not curse.

ROMANS 12:14 NKJV

Jesus prayed, "Forgive us our sins, for we also forgive everyone who is indebted to us."

LUKE 11:4 NKJV

Repay no one evil for evil. Have regard for good things in the sight of all men.

ROMANS 12:17 NKJV

Joseph told them, "Don't be afraid of me. Am I God, to judge and punish you?"

GENESIS 50:19 NLT

The past troubles will be forgotten and hidden from my eyes.

ISAIAH 65:16 NIV

It is a great thing to be a really good forgiver.

—F. W. BOREHAM

Everyone says forgiveness is a lovely idea, until they have something to forgive.

—C. S. LEWIS

Know and Grow

A wise man is strong, yes, a man of knowledge increases strength.

—*Proverbs 24:5 NKJV*

An old adage says, Knowledge is power. In the business world, this statement seems to ring true. The more you know, the more likely you'll make good decisions that lead to success rather than to failure.

A similar thing can be said about knowledge and Christian faith. The greater your knowledge, the more likely you'll make good decisions that lead to a fulfilling life. Knowledge is a good thing. And it's not just what you know, but it's also how you apply what you know.

Proverbs has a lot to say about knowledge and wisdom. Wisdom is given the highest of accolades and acknowledged as something worth pursuing, but knowledge isn't ignored, for without knowledge, wisdom is difficult to come by.

Growing knowledge in the context of Christian faith is not limited to an examination of the Bible, but that's a great place to start. Through casual as well as intense individual Bible study, you can learn more about the history of faith as well as the character of God. As you become familiar with the Bible, you'll learn where to turn when you need inspiration, redirection, or answers to difficult life questions. The more you study the Bible, the more truth you'll uncover that can help you navigate through life.

Small group study is nearly as critical as individual Bible study for building knowledge. By exploring the Bible and its truths in a group setting, you'll discover a wealth of new insights as other people share their unique perspectives. Scripture passages that have been difficult to understand can open up to new meaning through the perspective of another person. Challenge yourself and your Bible study partners to dig deep into the Scriptures together. You may want to have additional Bible study resources to refer to such as a Bible dictionary, a concordance, and perhaps some Bible commentaries.

Attend church, Sunday school, or independent Bible study classes regularly. While church attendance born out of repetition or duty may have limited merit, the real reason to attend is a desire to learn. Even if you're hearing the same sermon for the fourth time, there may be a nuance or a lesson yet to discover.

Be observant. Look around you. Some of the greatest education comes from experiencing life. Reflect on past lessons learned. Anticipate new lessons. Keep growing in knowledge, and you'll gain strength to move confidently through life.

I Will

Understand that there is great value in increasing knowledge.

yes ___ no ___

Know that greater knowledge of the Bible can help me find direction.

yes ___ no ___

Attempt to grow knowledge through Bible study.

yes ___ no ___

Develop a deeper understanding of faith through small group studies.

yes ___ no ___

Endeavor to learn more about faith through regular church attendance.

yes ___ no ___

Look for life lessons through everyday experiences.

yes ___ no ___

Things to Do

☐ *Ask God to increase my understanding of faith.*

☐ *Prepare a plan for regular Bible reading.*

☐ *Invite a Christian friend or two to meet regularly for Bible study.*

☐ *Study the book of Proverbs and learn about both the positive and negative aspects of pursuing knowledge.*

☐ *Purchase or borrow a book on how to do Bible study and read it.*

☐ *List five things you learned about life in the past week. Add any insights these lessons may have concerning faith.*

☐ *Choose one faith-related subject you'd like to learn more about and ask a pastor for recommendations of resources you can explore on that topic.*

Things to Remember

Do your best to add these things to your lives: to your faith, add goodness; and to your goodness, add knowledge.

2 PETER 1:5 NCV

This I pray, that your love may abound still more and more in knowledge and all discernment.

PHILIPPIANS 1:9 NKJV

I believe in your commands; now teach me good judgment and knowledge.

PSALM 119:66 NLT

My people have gone into captivity, because they have no knowledge; their honorable men are famished, and their multitude dried up with thirst.

ISAIAH 5:13 NKJV

The LORD said, "My people are destroyed for lack of knowledge. Because you have rejected knowledge, I also will reject you from being priest for Me; because you have forgotten the law of your God, I also will forget your children."

HOSEA 4:6 NKJV

All men naturally desire to know, but what doth knowledge avail without the fear of God?

—THOMAS À KEMPIS

If you have knowledge, let others light their candles at it.

—MARGARET FULLER

Reputation

Do You Know Me?

A good name is to be chosen rather than great riches, loving favor rather than silver and gold.

—Proverbs 22:1 NKJV

A restaurant lives or dies by its reputation. A great location and the promise of good food might bring customers into the restaurant once, but positive word-of-mouth brings in the all-important repeat business. Conversely, negative word-of-mouth can close a restaurant down. That's the clout of reputation.

That same clout can influence the way people respond to you. A good reputation brings people to your side and builds great, long-lasting relationships. A bad reputation sends people away or simply keeps them from looking to you for friendship in the first place.

The significance of having a good reputation is not lost in Scripture. Proverbs makes the daring comparison of wealth and reputation, with good reputation coming out on top as most desirable. In more subtle ways, the New Testament records how Paul sought out and recommended people of good reputation for key roles in the early church.

A good reputation can't be bought. It can only be earned over time. To earn a good reputation, follow Jesus' example. Jesus was honest and straightforward with people. When you speak the truth in love, you earn respect. Deception, or even polite half-truths eat away at a good reputation.

Follow through on what you say you're going to do. If you make a commitment, stick to it. People will learn that your word is good, that you keep your promises. Consistency speaks volumes to people who are so used to the unpredictability of a world built on the if-it-doesn't-work-try-something-else philosophy.

Know when to hold your tongue. Look for the good in a given situation. Speak well of others whenever you can do so honestly. If you can't, heed this time-honored advice: "If you don't have something good to say, don't say anything at all." Hurtful words have a way of finding their target when you express them among friends or even strangers. Be sure not to name names when you're talking. Keep in mind that your reputation is on the line with every word you speak.

Ultimately, if you base your actions and attitudes on Jesus' teachings, you'll be heading in the right direction. Jesus' life on earth was all about loving others. When you live according to this principle of love—and remain dependable with your love—others will learn to look at you with respect and you will earn a good reputation.

I Will

Examine what the Bible teaches about a good
reputation.   ___ yes   ___ no

Know that if I seek to be like Jesus, I will earn a
good reputation.   ___ yes   ___ no

Endeavor to be honest and straightforward with
people.   ___ yes   ___ no

Follow-through on those things I say I'm going
to do.   ___ yes   ___ no

Know that a good reputation is something to
strive for.   ___ yes   ___ no

Understand that earning a good reputation takes
time.   ___ yes   ___ no

Things to Do

☐ Ask God to help you know what it means to have a good reputation.

☐ Study Jesus' Sermon on the Mount in Matthew 5 and 6 and explore
how these teachings can help you develop a good reputation.

☐ Ask a few close friends to evaluate your reputation.

☐ Read a biography about someone you think has a good reputation.

☐ Write down any habits or attitudes you may need to change in order to
earn a good reputation.

☐ Visit a restaurant that has a great reputation and one with a not-so-
great reputation. Apply what you learn about reputation to your own
life.

Things to Remember

The governors and satraps sought to find some charge against Daniel concerning the kingdom; but they could find no charge or fault, because he was faithful; nor was there any error or fault found in him.

DANIEL 6:4 NKJV

Seek out from among you seven men of good reputation, full of the Holy Spirit and wisdom, whom we may appoint over this business.

ACTS 6:3 NKJV

He was well spoken of by the brethren who were at Lystra and Iconium. Paul wanted to have him go on with him.

ACTS 16:2–3 NKJV

We are also sending another brother with Titus. He is highly praised in all the churches as a preacher of the Good News.

2 CORINTHIANS 8:18 NLT

A good name is better than precious ointment.

ECCLESIASTES 7:1 NKJV

Like a bird that wanders from its nest is a man who wanders from his place.

PROVERBS 27:8 NKJV

Reputation is but a signboard to show where virtue lodges.

—SAINT FRANCIS DE SALES

Character is what you are in the dark.

—DWIGHT L. MOODY

Fighting Fear

Creator Comforts

We may boldly say: "The Lord is my helper; I will not fear. What can man do to me?"

—*Hebrews 13:6* NKJV

Shadows shifting unpredictably in an already-dark room. Footfalls echoing behind you in a long, dimly lit alleyway. The sudden slamming of a door in an empty house. Are you afraid? Hollywood would like you to be. Movies love to prey on people's fears. And for some reason, people like to be scared. Perhaps that's because, in a movie theater, everyone knows instinctively that the danger isn't real. It's a safe place to be afraid.

Life outside the theater, however, isn't always safe. There is little question these days that evil is real. People do hurt other people. Safety is never really fully assured, no matter what measures are taken to protect you. And there are other fears. Fear of heights. Fear of flying. Fear of the dark. All these are real fears too. The list is long.

Fear can be a good thing. It can force you to move cautiously. It can help you to stay focused and can clue you in to the inherent danger of a given situation. But if fear starts to run your life, it becomes a bad thing. When fear grips you and won't let go, you are immobilized. Life can't continue as normal because there is no normal.

There is good news. You don't have to be ruled by fear. You have a powerful ally—the Creator of the universe. Throughout the Bible, God's people struggled with being afraid. While in captivity in Egypt, the Israelites feared for their safety. Even as they escaped Egypt, they feared for their lives knowing the Egyptian army followed close behind. The ever-present threat of war kept fear in their hearts for centuries. Yet through all of these times, God promised to be near.

God is still near. As the writer of Hebrews pointed out in his quote from Psalm 118:6, God is also your helper. Mere men cannot match His power. This truth is the cornerstone for overcoming fear. God is greater than your enemy—whether that enemy lives in the real world or in your mind.

Prayer is one of the greatest weapons against fear. In prayer, you connect with God's power and presence. Sometimes all it takes is a simple prayer of "Help" or "Calm me" to overcome fear. Other times, fervent prayer can help you discover a different answer to your fear. Learn to live each day with an attitude of prayer. This constant, wherever-you-are connection with God can help to thwart the possibility of fear as you come to know God's nearness in all of life's circumstances.

God's Word is also an excellent place to turn when you're scared. The Bible is packed with Scriptures of comfort. If it is possible, carry a small Bible with you. That way you can flip open to reassuring passages when faced with fear. Memorize a few of your favorite calming passages so they'll be on the tip of your tongue when trepidation shows up.

Know that God is in control even when the lights are out. Fear is really all about darkness and the unknown. But no matter how little you know about any given situation, God can see the whole thing. He is more powerful than any evil you might face. That doesn't mean you'll never suffer at the hands of evil or the object of your fear—but it does mean that God won't leave you alone in fear.

Look beyond the situation whenever possible. Most times of fearfulness are temporary. Can you see the proverbial light at the end of the tunnel? Look down the road past the point of dread and draw strength from a soon-to-come moment that will be free from fear.

Seek comfort and support from others. Fear that is kept in isolation can grow bigger than it really is. Invite close friends to help you with your fears. Ask them to stand beside you. With their words of wisdom and encouragement, you can knock your fear down to a manageable size or even destroy it.

Face your fears with confidence. God conquered death and will defeat evil too. Justice will come. Faithfulness will be rewarded. Trust God's greater plan and move courageously through life.

When the men of Israel saw the vast number of enemy troops,
they lost their nerve entirely and tried to hide
in caves, holes, rocks, tombs, and cisterns.
—1 Samuel 13:6 NKJV

I Will

Look to God's Word for comfort. *yes* *no*

Face fear confidently knowing that God is ultimately in control. *yes* *no*

Trust that God is always near and is greater than any evil I might face. *yes* *no*

Learn to have an attitude of prayer and to pray often when afraid. *yes* *no*

Know that life isn't guaranteed to be free from danger. *yes* *no*

Realize there are positive aspects to fear. *yes* *no*

Things to Do

☐ *List your top five fears.*

☐ *Choose one of those fears and ask God to help you overcome it.*

☐ *Choose a favorite comforting Bible passage and memorize it.*

☐ *Invite a friend for coffee and talk together about your fears and how to deal with them.*

☐ *Interview a few people about their greatest fears. Ask these people how they overcome fear.*

☐ *Write a note to God, thanking Him for promising to always be near.*

☐ *Copy four or five relevant Scripture passages onto a sheet of paper you can carry with you.*

Things to Remember

Jacob prayed, "Deliver me, I pray, from the hand of my brother, from the hand of Esau; for I fear him, lest he come and attack me and the mother with the children."

GENESIS 32:11 NKJV

At this rate they were afraid we would soon be driven against the rocks along the shore, so they threw out four anchors from the stern and prayed for daylight.

ACTS 27:29 NKJV

So Adam said, "I heard Your voice in the garden, and I was afraid because I was naked; and I hid myself."
—Genesis 3:10 NKJV

The guards shook for fear of him, and became like dead men. But the angel answered and said to the women, "Do not be afraid, for I know that you seek Jesus who was crucified."

MATTHEW 28:4–5 NKJV

The same day at evening, being the first day of the week, when the doors were shut where the disciples were assembled, for fear of the Jews, Jesus came and stood in the midst, and said to them, "Peace be with you."

JOHN 20:19 NKJV

Upon arrival in Jerusalem he tried to meet with the believers, but they were all afraid of him. They thought he was faking!

ACTS 9:26 TLB

Jesus said, "People will faint from fear and foreboding of what is coming upon the world, for the powers of the heavens will be shaken."

LUKE 21:26 NRSV

The wicked flee when no one pursues, but the righteous are bold as a lion.

PROVERBS 28:1 NKJV

The LORD said, "Like adamant stone, harder than flint, I have made your forehead; do not be afraid of them, nor be dismayed at their looks, though they are a rebellious house."

EZEKIEL 3:9 NKJV

Moreover David said, "The LORD, who delivered me from the paw of the lion and from the paw of the bear, He will deliver me from the hand of this Philistine." And Saul said to David, "Go, and the LORD be with you!"

1 SAMUEL 17:37 NKJV

Fear is a conglomeration of sinister shadows, and a shadow that has no substance.

—NORMAN VINCENT PEALE

Though this world with devils filled should threaten to undo us we will not fear for God has willed His truth to triumph through us.

—MARTIN LUTHER

Dealing with Loss

No Unheard Cries

The LORD said: "I have surely seen the oppression of My people who are in Egypt, and have heard their cry because of their taskmasters, for I know their sorrows."

—Exodus 3:7 NKJV

The losses you've experienced in life make lasting impressions. Moving away from longtime friends; losing a loved one to cancer; watching a child run away from God. All these circumstances can significantly imprint your heart. Where once joy lived, emptiness reigns. It can take a long time for that emptiness to disappear.

As a people, the Israelites experienced all kinds of loss. Once enslaved in Egypt, they dealt with the loss of their homeland, their freedom, and their very identity. But God heard their cries and their sorrows. He knew His plan would soon take them out of slavery, but while they remained, He held them in His arms and captured their tears.

God's role in your experience of loss is very much the same as it was in Old Testament times. He knows what lies ahead for you; He knows what life looks like after the emptiness. He hears your cries. And He stands beside you while you endure the hurt. Though you may believe you're the only one who feels the way you do after a loss, you are not alone. God is with you and He understands your pain; He suffered the loss of His son, Jesus, on the cross.

After Jesus' death but before the truth of his resurrection was known, the disciples spent time together. In part, this may have been because they feared for their lives. But it is just as likely they needed one another's company to deal with their loss. There are appropriate times to be alone when you hurt, but you also need the comfort of friends. Find someone who will be patient with your anger. Choose friends who can simply be there for you. You may need to yell or scream, or you may just want to cry. Close friends who know you well will ride the wave of your emotions with you.

When you lose someone close to you, you may go through different stages of grief. You may not want to believe that the person is gone. You may become angry. You may feel deep sadness. Eventually, you may come to accept that things are going to be different. Each of these stages is important and valid and normal. Each has a role in the healing process. One of the most powerful verses in the Bible is also one of the shortest. John 11:35 recounted Jesus' response to the loss of a friend. It reads simply: "Jesus wept." It's okay to cry.

I Will

Trust that God will be near in my time of loss.   *yes*   *no*

Believe God hears my cries when I am hurting.   *yes*   *no*

Know that I will likely face loss during my life.   *yes*   *no*

Understand that it's normal to go through anger or denial when I've suffered a loss.   *yes*   *no*

Seek the comfort of friends when I'm in pain.   *yes*   *no*

Recognize that God knows what it's like to suffer loss.   *yes*   *no*

Know that it's okay to cry when I've suffered a loss.   *yes*   *no*

Things to Do

☐ *Ask God for strength and wisdom to face any loss you've recently experienced.*

☐ *Go for a walk and spend the quiet time thinking about what it means to suffer loss and how God's nearness can help.*

☐ *Study John 20 and consider what feelings the disciples might have gone through after Jesus' death.*

☐ *Recall a time when you suffered a loss; write down the feelings you went through.*

☐ *Call a friend you know is dealing with a loss and offer to help in any way you can.*

☐ *Pick up a book on how to grieve and read it.*

Things to Remember

The ropes of death wrapped around me. The traps of death were before me. In my trouble I called to the Lord. I cried out to my God for help. From his temple he heard my voice; my call for help reached his ears.

PSALM 18:5–6 NCV

Jesus said, "Are you inquiring among yourselves about what I said, 'A little while, and you will not see Me; and again a little while, and you will see Me'? Most assuredly, I say to you that you will weep and lament, but the world will rejoice; and you will be sorrowful, but your sorrow will be turned into joy."

JOHN 16:19–20 NKJV

[The elders of the church] all wept freely, and fell on Paul's neck and kissed him, sorrowing most of all for the words which he spoke, that they would see his face no more. And they accompanied him to the ship.

ACTS 20:37–38 NKJV

He will swallow up death forever, and the Lord GOD will wipe away tears from all faces; the rebuke of His people He will take away from all the earth; for the LORD has spoken.

ISAIAH 25:8 NKJV

God whispers in our pleasures but shouts in our pain.

—C. S. LEWIS

There is no grief which time does not lessen and soften.

—MARCUS TULLIUS CICERO

Responsible Freedom

Within Limits

Beware lest somehow this liberty of yours become a stumbling block to those who are weak.

—1 Corinthians 8:9 NKJV

Do anything you want. Anywhere. Anytime. Sound like freedom? Well, it might be if you were the only person in a perfect world. But you're not. Your life intersects with others. What you do can have an impact on someone else's life. That's why freedom comes with responsibility. Imagine what might happen if everyone exercised the freedom of racing around city streets at full speed with no regard for each other. Laws and rules are necessary to protect freedom.

There is another kind of freedom that Paul talked about in the Bible, and it carries a similar kind of responsibility. This is the freedom that accompanies a relationship with Christ. You are set free when you become a Christian. What does that mean? It means you are freed from the power of sin. It also means you are no longer shackled to the laws that used to determine a path to God, laws that became twisted as the Israelites layered law upon law, making a relationship with God impossible.

In 1 Corinthians 8:9 Paul spoke to the Corinthian church about the members' confusion regarding meat that had once been offered to idols. Previously, the law had prohibited them from eating the meat. But since they were now free from the law, eating this meat suddenly looked like a good idea. Paul's caution, however, illustrates the responsibility that comes with freedom in Christ. Choosing to do something that might harm another could be irresponsible, even if it is allowed.

Being responsible with your freedom begins with a concern for others. If you know well the people who surround you at work, home, school, or elsewhere, then you probably know what kinds of things might be inappropriate to do around them. Be logical and practical, and choose your actions and words carefully when the subject matter could be considered controversial.

Opt for the conservative choice over the radical one when among other Christians. Freedom in Christ may mean something different to you than to another Christian. Respect other people's beliefs by showing restraint with your words and actions.

In all you do, keep the focus on your relationship with God. Irresponsible use of freedom usually flows out of selfishness or a lack of concern for what's right. When you run every potentially controversial act through the what-would-God-have-me-do filter, you reduce the likelihood of abusing your freedom and causing someone to stumble or question their faith.

I Will

Know that I am free in Christ when I become a
Christian.   *yes*   *no*

Know that freedom in Christ may mean something
different to another person.   *yes*   *no*

Understand that freedom comes with responsibility.   *yes*   *no*

Consider what is right to do in any given situation.   *yes*   *no*

Examine what it means to live responsibly.   *yes*   *no*

Show concern for others by the way I act around
them.   *yes*   *no*

Choose word and actions carefully.   *yes*   *no*

Things to Do

☐ *Study Romans 6:18 and consider what it means to be a "slave to
righteousness."*

☐ *Talk with a close friend about appropriate boundaries for freedom.*

☐ *Write down what it means to you to be free in Christ.*

☐ *Talk with a pastor or other church leader about the responsibility that
comes with freedom.*

☐ *Make a list of new opportunities that come with freedom in Christ.*

☐ *Write down four or five dangers of being irresponsible with freedom.*

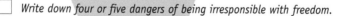

Things to Remember

Jesus said, "If the Son makes you free, you shall be free indeed."

JOHN 8:36 NKJV

You have been set free from sin and have become slaves to righteousness.

ROMANS 6:18 NIV

You are not slaves; you are free. But your freedom is not an excuse to do evil. You are free to live as God's slaves.

1 PETER 2:16 NKJV

Stand fast therefore in the liberty by which Christ has made us free, and do not be entangled again with a yoke of bondage.

GALATIANS 5:1 NKJV

Having been set free from sin, and having become slaves of God, you have your fruit to holiness, and the end, everlasting life.

ROMANS 6:22 NKJV

Once you were under God's curse, doomed forever for your sins.

EPHESIANS 2:1 TLB

Freedom! No word was ever spoken that has held greater hope, demanded greater sacrifice, needed more to be nurtured, blessed more the giver . . . or came closer to being God's will on earth.

—OMAR N. BRADLEY

There are two freedoms—the false, where a man is free to do what he likes; and the true, where a man is free to do what he ought.

—CHARLES KINGSLEY

Better than You Can Dream

I saw a new heaven and a new earth, for the first heaven and the first earth had passed away. Also there was no more sea. Then I, John, saw the holy city, New Jerusalem, coming down out of heaven from God, prepared as a bride adorned for her husband.

—Revelation 21:1–2 NKJV

Popular culture's acceptance of the idea of heaven has been almost universal in scope. Heaven shows up in movies, music, television, and just about any other form of media. The word itself has become synonymous with *fantastic* or *wonderful* and is used often in everyday conversations. Like few words in the English language, *heaven* is void of any negative connotations. It's a word that paints a picture of beauty, hope, and love.

Christians and non-Christians alike talk about heaven with a mixture of self-assurance and bewilderment. Though people who know Christ may understand what the Bible says about getting into heaven, most non-Christians probably only have the general idea that heaven is a retirement home in the sky for people who were good on earth.

The Bible clearly points the way to heaven, and it's only through a relationship with Christ. This can be a sobering thought when you consider all those people who choose not to follow God. But there is little debate on this topic. What is heaven like? And how much thought should you give it while still on earth?

Heaven is oft depicted in illustrations as being a field of clouds in the sky where angels float around and play harps all day. Maybe you see gold-paved streets or a green, flower-filled field. Some people picture heaven as being something like a new version of the paradise God created way back in the beginning—but this time, without the snake. The Bible doesn't offer many specifics about what heaven will look like. What it does offer is this: Heaven is a real place, not just some communal dream state. It's a place of beauty beyond compare. And it's the place where all who love God will live forever.

That word *forever* brings up a million questions about heaven. Few, if any, will ever be answered while you're here on earth. Heaven remains one of the most mysterious components of God's plan. But that very mystery is what makes heaven such a compelling topic of discussion. What will it be like to be in God's presence? (Indescribable, certainly, in human terms.) Will you recognize loved ones? (Probably, and you'll still be you.) Then there are the fun questions. Will you be able to fly? Run faster? Swim underwater for an hour? The questions are often mind-numbing. But the promises of heaven are enough to make up for that which you don't yet know.

One of the promises of heaven is that it will be free of pain and suffering. For many people, this alone is enough to draw them toward a relationship with God. But it is possible to have your head stuck in the clouds as it were always thinking of heaven, and forget to live while here on earth. God wants you to have a fulfilling life on earth too. Sometimes you may need to glance at the future promise of heaven to get through a tough time. Go ahead. Just don't forget to bring your gaze back to earth.

Another promise is that you'll have a new body. No one quite knows what that means, but it's got to be a good thing. It's not just your old body you'll be leaving behind: You won't be bringing along any earthly riches to heaven, either. The only thing you can bring with you is the influence you have had on others here on earth in leading them to Christ. Surely there is no more fulfilling role you could play than to point others to heaven's gate.

Heaven is an incredible place. When you consider all it has to offer—and the fact that it's likely far greater than you can imagine—it's a wonder anyone chooses to stay on earth. Even the apostle Paul grappled with this, telling the Philippian church he honestly struggled sometimes as he considered and compared life on earth and life with Jesus in heaven. But like Paul, you were placed here on earth for a reason. You have a life to live and a God to get to know. Yes, heaven is a real and desirable place to be. Only God knows what day is scheduled for your reservation. Until then, live life, love God, and know that a fantastic future awaits.

I lift my eyes to you, O God, enthroned in heaven.
—PSLAM 123:1 NLT

I Will

Know that heaven is a real place.
    yes   *no*

Believe that heaven is a far better place than I can imagine.
    yes   *no*

Explore what it means to live with the hope of heaven.
    yes   *no*

Accept that it's important to live life fully on earth and not dwell on the future hope of heaven.
    yes   *no*

Recognize that only God knows when it is my turn to enter heaven.
    yes   *no*

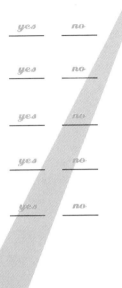

Things to Do

☐ *Thank God for the gift of heaven.*

☐ *Invite a few Christian friends over for dessert and spend time together dreaming of what heaven might be like.*

☐ *List five things you're looking forward to about heaven.*

☐ *List five things you enjoy about life on earth.*

☐ *Find two or three songs about heaven and listen to them. Consider how the songs' messages compare to your understanding of heaven.*

☐ *Interview a few small children, asking them what they think heaven will be like.*

☐ *Draw a picture, write a poem, or choose some other creative activity to depict the joy of heaven.*

Things to Remember

We are already God's children, right now, and we can't even imagine what it is going to be like later on. But we do know this, that when he comes we will be like him, as a result of seeing him as he really is.

1 John 3:2 TLB

Jesus said, "Indeed they cannot die anymore, because they are like angels and are children of God, being children of the resurrection."

Luke 20:36 NRSV

Blessed are those who do His commandments, that they may have the right to the tree of life, and may enter through the gates into the city.
—Revelation 22:14 NKJV

Paul wrote: Behold, I tell you a mystery: We shall not all sleep, but we shall all be changed—in a moment, in the twinkling of an eye, at the last trumpet. For the trumpet will sound, and the dead will be raised incorruptible, and we shall be changed.

1 Corinthians 15:51–52 NKJV

The Lamb on the Throne will shepherd them, will lead them to spring waters of Life. And God will wipe every last tear from their eyes.

Revelation 7:17 THE MESSAGE

He, being full of the Holy Spirit, gazed into heaven and saw the glory of God, and Jesus standing at the right hand of God.

ACTS 7:55 NKJV

I am hard pressed between the two, having a desire to depart and be with Christ, which is far better.

PHILIPPIANS 1:23 NKJV

The one sitting on the throne said, "Look, I am making all things new!" And then he said to me, "Write this down, for what I tell you is trustworthy and true."

REVELATION 21:5 NKJV

But now we groan in this tent. We want God to give us our heavenly home.

2 CORINTHIANS 5:2 NCV

Jesus said, "Sell what you have and give alms; provide yourselves money bags which do not grow old, a treasure in the heavens that does not fail, where no thief approaches nor moth destroys."

LUKE 12:33 NKJV

Aim at Heaven and you will get earth "thrown in": aim at earth and you will get neither.

—C. S. LEWIS

Heaven: where questions and answers become one.

—ELIE WIESEL

Building Instructions

I said to the nobles, the rulers, and the rest of the people, "The work is great and extensive, and we are separated far from one another on the wall. Wherever you hear the sound of the trumpet, rally to us there. Our God will fight for us."

—Nehemiah 4:19–20 NKJV

Many of the great accomplishments in history began as one person's vision or dream. But few of those accomplishments would have materialized without the support and encouragement of others. The role of encouragement cannot be underestimated. Imagine an inventor struggling to solve a problem with his new invention. Or a parent wrestling with the challenge of raising a temperamental teenager. The support of others greatly improves their chances for success.

The Israelites faced a true test when they began to rebuild the walls following their return to Jerusalem. Each day as they endeavored to build the wall—a monumental construction project—they faced the imminent threat of enemy nations and the obstacle of limited resources. Morale dropped. But their leader, Nehemiah, kept encouraging the people. He calmed their fears of being attacked by placing families on guard where the wall had yet to be completed. His strategy was brilliant. The workers regained their confidence, the enemies gave up their threat, and the wall was completed in fifty-two days.

Without Nehemiah's encouragement, the Israelites might have never finished the wall. What made his encouragement effective, however, wasn't necessarily the words he spoke, but the love for his people. Love is the cornerstone of encouragement.

When you truly love someone, your words of support for that person are full of significance and make a meaningful difference. Love also compels you to walk beside someone rather than to wave and to cheer from a distance. The commitment to partner with them in the middle of the struggle generates optimism and fuels the possibility of success.

Supporting others also means spending time together. Listening to their frustrations. Offering words of support. Letting people know that even though you can't always be with them, you will be praying for them.

Sometimes encouragers must redirect those they wish to uplift. When a friend chooses an impossible path, your role may be to gently redirect that person. Your encouragement to try a new idea or approach can save the person from repeatedly hitting a wall. As long as your redirection is born out of concern and love, your words will make a difference.

One of the most important responsibilities of an encourager is that of reminding. People who face challenges need to be reminded that God is near. They need to be reminded that others have gone before them and been victorious, and they need to be reminded that you believe in them. Your encouragement can breathe fresh hope into a circumstance that was once decorated with despair.

I Will

Learn to pray for others who are in need and to spend time with them whenever I can.

_____ yes _____ no

Know that encouragement helps others to succeed.

_____ yes _____ no

Realize the value of encouragement for those who are facing a challenging situation.

_____ yes _____ no

Understand that true encouragement is anchored in love.

_____ yes _____ no

Recognize that walking alongside someone in support is better than cheering from the sidelines.

_____ yes _____ no

Examine the function of redirection as it relates to encouragement.

_____ yes _____ no

Things to Do

- [ ] *Read Colossians and see how Paul used encouragement to help grow the early church.*

- [ ] *Study how Nehemiah encouraged others to rebuild the temple in Nehemiah 1–6.*

- [ ] *Call a friend you know is facing a challenge and offer encouragement.*

- [ ] *Write yourself a reminder note outlining basic truths you ought to remember when you feel discouraged.*

- [ ] *Choose one way you can be supportive of a person or group of people you work with and follow through on your idea.*

- [ ] *Visit the library or go online and read a magazine article about an inventor or another person who accomplished something great. See what you can find about how the person received encouragement.*

Things to Remember

We are happy to be weak, if you are strong, and we pray that you will become complete.

2 CORINTHIANS 13:9 NCV

I rejoice that I have confidence in you in everything.

2 CORINTHIANS 7:16 NKJV

Elisha answered, "Do not fear, for those who are with us are more than those who are with them."

2 KINGS 6:16 NKJV

Show respect for everyone. Love Christians everywhere.

1 PETER 2:17 TLB

Preach the word! Be ready in season and out of season. Convince, rebuke, exhort, with all longsuffering and teaching.

2 TIMOTHY 4:2 NKJV

Jonathan said to David, "Do not fear, for the hand of Saul my father shall not find you. You shall be king over Israel, and I shall be next to you. Even my father Saul knows that."

1 SAMUEL 23:17 NKJV

Find the good and applaud.
—ZIG ZIGLAR

For every critical comment we receive, it takes nine affirming comments to even out the negative effect in our life.

—JIM BURNS

Spiritual Maturity

Turn the Page

Let us stop going over the basics of Christianity again and again. Let us go on instead and become mature in our understanding. Surely we don't need to start all over again with the importance of turning away from evil deeds and placing our faith in God.

—Hebrews 6:1 *NKJV*

One of the few inevitables in life is aging. Though beauty product manufacturers, plastic surgeons, and even some scientists might claim otherwise, no one has truly been able to fight the aging process. You are going to grow old. Still, many people wrestle aging with as much energy as they can muster.

You've probably heard someone say to a child, "act your age" in an attempt to curb age-inappropriate bad behavior. Some adults need to hear this too. The writer of Hebrews wrote similar words to the recipients of his letter. In it, he challenged readers to "stop acting like baby Christians and grow up!"

One of the benefits of aging is the accumulation of past experiences that can help a person make better decisions later in life. If you listen to what the past has taught, you can learn to be more patient, loving, and respectful (among other things). However, as evidenced in the book of Hebrews, sometimes people get stuck at a particular maturity level and don't seem to grow at all.

Acting one's age in a spiritual sense means gaining maturity. The greatest place to grow spiritual maturity is through Bible study. No matter how long you've been reading the Bible, there is always more to learn. Because life doesn't slow down, each time you explore God's Word, you come from a slightly different place emotionally, mentally, and spiritually. That changing perspective can lead to exciting new insights about God and what it means to live a life of faith. Immature Christians say, "I already know it all." Mature Christians say, "The more I learn, the more I learn about how much I don't know."

Another way to grow is to listen to or read about the life experience of others. One hallmark of spiritual maturity is the ability to interact confidently and politely with people who have different ideas about faith. Mature Christians know that acceptance of and love for others doesn't mean you endorse what they believe. But it does prompt you to listen and to be open to new ideas.

Patience is probably the most important ingredient in developing spiritual maturity. While there are ways to speed up your acquisition of knowledge, knowing what to do with that knowledge can take time. If you want to grow spiritually, be diligent in study, and patient with God.

I Will

Be patient with God as I seek to grow a mature
faith.

yes _no_

Accept that aging is inevitable in life.

yes _no_

Know that aging doesn't automatically mean
growing maturity.

yes _no_

Learn from past experience in order to develop
greater maturity.

yes _no_

Start each day with a desire to learn and grow.

yes _no_

Continue studying the Bible and anticipate greater
understanding.

yes _no_

Learn from the life experience of others.

yes _no_

Things to Do

☐ _Ask God to reveal something new the next time you read the Bible._

☐ _Study the book of Hebrews and look for new insights into what it
means to be a mature Christian._

☐ _Contact a longtime Christian—someone you see as having a mature
faith—and invite that person out to dinner. Ask lots of questions and
learn what you can about a growing faith._

☐ _On a sheet of paper, list the differences in your understanding of faith
between a time when you first knew Christ, and today._

☐ _Ask a pastor to share three or four ideas on how you can grow a
mature faith._

Things to Remember

Blessed are those who hunger and thirst for righteousness, for they shall be filled.
MATTHEW 5:6 NKJV

His delight is in the law of the Lord, and on his law he meditates day and night.
PSALM 1:2 NIV

You have been Christians a long time now, and you ought to be teaching others. Instead, you need someone to teach you again the basic things a beginner must learn about the Scriptures.
HEBREWS 5:12 NKJV

Now we see in a mirror, dimly, but then face to face. Now I know in part, but then I shall know just as I also am known.
1 CORINTHIANS 13:12 NKJV

Everyone who partakes only of milk is unskilled in the word of righteousness, for he is a babe.
HEBREWS 5:13 NKJV

Brethren, do not be children in understanding; however, in malice be babes, but in understanding be mature.
1 CORINTHIANS 14:20 NKJV

One of the marks of a mature person is the ability to dissent without creating dissension.
—DON ROBINSON

Spiritual maturity comes not by erudition, but by compliance with the known will of God.
—D. W. LAMBERT

Wind Chasing

I looked on all the works that my hands had done and on the labor in which I had toiled; and indeed all was vanity and grasping for the wind. There was no profit under the sun.

—*Ecclesiastes 2:11* NKJV

In the lifelong search for meaning, you may endure seasons when life seems to have no point. All your great deeds—your accomplishments at work, your success in relationships—suddenly seem like puffs of smoke. They're here for a moment, then gone. The author of Ecclesiastes must have had a moment like that when he wrote "all was vanity and grasping for the wind."

The writer of the Kansas song "Dust in the Wind" may have had a similar transcendent moment. The band's song was an instant hit with the public, quite possibly because so many people could relate to its groping-for-the-meaning-of-life lyrics. In moments like this, you realize you are here merely for a blip of time in the context of eternity. Your accomplishments, no matter how great among people, mean little or nothing in the broader scope of things. You are but dust in the wind, but only—and this is critical—when you look for your self-worth in earthly tasks and earthly relationships.

All people are created with a God-shaped hole that's waiting to be filled. When you try to fill that hole with anything other than God, such as worldly success or conquests, life never quite finds its purpose. Left unfilled, that God-shaped hole leaves a feeling of emptiness that comes and goes at will.

When you begin a relationship with God, life finds a purpose. Life begins to make sense, and the emptiness disappears. It's important to understand that just about everyone goes through the wilderness times. You're not alone when you feel empty inside.

Even when you come to know God, you may still find yourself feeling alone or lost at times. That doesn't mean God has left you. It may simply mean you have lost sight of God. When you have these moments, open the Bible. Read Ecclesiastes to remind yourself that you're not alone in your search for significance. Read Psalms to rediscover a range of experience in what it means to be in relationship with God. Then read the Gospel of John to see just how much Jesus loves you.

You may find yourself struggling still to know what your purpose is in life. A life's purpose may include some grand task, but it may also be in the details. Make it your life's work to grow closer to God and you'll uncover those details along the way.

I Will

Examine what it means to have a "God-shaped hole."

yes   *no*

Understand that a relationship with God gives life purpose.

yes   *no*

Be comforted to know that I am not alone in feeling lost or purposeless at times.

yes   *no*

Seek out God through the Bible when I have a hard time discovering meaning.

yes   *no*

Know that it's not unusual to feel at times like life has no purpose.

yes   *no*

Consider that my purpose in life may not be a single task, but the way in which I live.

yes   *no*

Things to Do

☐ *Read the entire book of Ecclesiastes and reflect on the author's examination of the difference between life without God and life that's centered on God.*

☐ *Ask God to help you see the real meaning of life in practical ways.*

☐ *Listen to the song "Dust in the Wind" and consider what its message says about the purpose of life.*

☐ *Interview five people at random and ask the question, "Where do you find your significance in life?"*

☐ *Think of three ways in which God has used you to have an impact on the lives of others.*

Things to Remember

Whatever is born of God overcomes the world. And this is the victory that has overcome the world—our faith.

1 JOHN 5:4 NKJV

There is no condemnation for those who belong to Christ Jesus.

ROMANS 8:1 NKJV

In all these things we are more than conquerors through Him who loved us.

ROMANS 8:37 NKJV

God has given me the wonderful privilege of telling everyone about this plan of his; and he has given me his power and special ability to do it well.

EPHESIANS 3:7 TLB

Who knows what is good for man in life, all the days of his vain life which he passes like a shadow? Who can tell a man what will happen after him under the sun?

ECCLESIASTES 6:12 NKJV

Jesus said, "Most assuredly, I say to you, he who believes in Me, the works that I do he will do also; and greater works than these he will do, because I go to My Father."

JOHN 14:12 NKJV

> Life is filled with meaning as soon as Jesus Christ enters into it.
>
> —STEPHEN NEILL

> Living a good, decent, Christian life is what's important; live that life and the rest will follow.
>
> —SPIKE MILLIGAN

Pass the Tissues

God comforts us in all our troubles so that we can comfort others. When others are troubled, we will be able to give them the same comfort God has given us.

—*2 Corinthians 1:4* NLT

One of the greatest promises of heaven is that there will no longer be any pain or suffering. To someone who is hurting today, however, that promise may offer little comfort. The immediacy of pain is not easily ignored or deferred (nor should it be). When someone hurts right now, right now is when that person needs comfort.

That's where you come in. In Paul's letter to the Corinthians, he made special reference to the value of God's comfort and how it ought to inspire people to comfort one another. Rather than give trite advice such as "be there for each other," as so many people do today, Paul gave specific guidance, saying, "Comfort others just as God comforts you."

One of the only sure things you can count about the future is that God will comfort you. Knowing this brings a sense of peace even in difficult times. In a similar way, you can be there with comfort for someone who hurts.

Sometimes just the knowledge that you're only a phone call away is enough to get a person through a tough time.

God also offers a listening ear to those who are in need through the vehicle of prayer. In a like manner, you can offer your willingness to listen to a hurting friend. Often one of the most important steps to overcoming a hurtful experience is talking about it. When you sit with a hurting person and listen, you provide comfort and help move along the all-important process of grieving.

It's not uncommon for people to suffer needlessly or to allow suffering to go on too long. Sometimes God steers you in a new direction when you're stuck in a cycle of pain. There are times when you'll need to provide this same redirection for someone who is hurting. But if the person's pain is causing him or her to make dangerous choices, you may need to take bolder action and step in the way of a bad decision.

But whether you are simply available to a friend or are taking an active role in helping that friend move beyond the pain, the most important thing to do is love that person. God's love is immeasurable and doesn't go away. Your friend may welcome your help or push you away, but the single greatest thing you can continue to do for someone who is hurting is to love that person, no matter what the circumstance. Draw from God's love as much as necessary, and offer it to someone in need of comfort.

I Will

Understand that I ought to comfort others as God comforts me.

    yes   _no_

Know that people are going to suffer pain and hurt.

    yes   _no_

Recognize that people who are hurting can benefit from my comfort.

    yes   _no_

Learn to be available for someone who is hurting.

    yes   _no_

Offer to listen when someone needs to share about a painful experience.

    yes   _no_

Help redirect a friend who is hurting when it's best to do so.

    yes   _no_

Things to Do

- ☐ *Ask God to give you the sensitivity to know when you ought to reach out to a hurting friend.*

- ☐ *Write out ways God has comforted you in the past, then consider how you can offer similar methods of comfort to others.*

- ☐ *Write a note to a friend who is hurting, offering your availability to listen to that person.*

- ☐ *Recall a time when you were hurting and think of the ways others helped you through that experience.*

- ☐ *Invite a friend to tell what kinds of things have helped him or her go through hurtful times.*

Things to Remember

God, who comforts the downcast, comforted us by the coming of Titus, and not only by his coming, but also by the consolation with which he was comforted in you, when he told us of your earnest desire, your mourning, your zeal for me, so that I rejoiced even more.

2 CORINTHIANS 7:6–7 NKJV

You should forgive him and comfort him to keep him from having too much sadness and giving up completely.

2 CORINTHIANS 2:7 NCV

"Comfort, yes, comfort My people!" says your God.

ISAIAH 40:1 NKJV

Whatever things were written before were written for our learning, that we through the patience and comfort of the Scriptures might have hope.

ROMANS 15:4 NKJV

Praise be to the God and Father of our Lord Jesus Christ. God is the Father who is full of mercy and all comfort.

2 CORINTHIANS 1:3 NCV

Jesus went without comfort so that he could send us the Comforter.

—EDITH SCHAEFFER

God does not comfort us to make us comfortable, but to make us comforters.

—JOHN HENRY JOWETT

God's Love

Arms that Circle the Universe

God so loved the world, that he gave his only begotten Son, that whosoever believeth in him should not perish, but have everlasting life.

—John 3:16 KJV

Think big, really big. This evening, glance outside at the homes and buildings in your neighborhood. Then look to the horizon and the lights that betray the breadth of your town or city. Look at the night sky. Use your imagination to see beyond the solar system, the Milky Way galaxy, and even farther—to the stars that no one has even seen yet. Now draw a box around all you can imagine.

God's love is bigger. But a love so big is incomprehensible. So God chose to show His love in a way that humanity might understand: He sent His Son, Jesus, to die on the cross so that people could have everlasting life.

The concept of sacrifice is foreign to many people. Some might think that handing the remote control to a spouse or child is a sacrifice. Others might see giving up a favorite food as a sacrifice. But real sacrifice costs much more than a moment of inconvenience.

In Old Testament times, the Israelites sacrificed animals to honor God. But as humanity stumbled and slipped farther and farther away from God, the sacrifices meant less and less. Sin ruled and separated God from people. In God's great plan, there was only one way to bring the people back to Him: the ultimate sacrifice of His own Son.

Because of God's great love for humanity, Jesus died on the cross. But Jesus didn't just die, He defeated death and opened up a path to the Father once again. God's love is big enough to circle the universe and small enough to be focused just on you.

God's love is a personal love. He wants to have a unique relationship with you. When you pray, ask God to reveal Himself to you. Simply say, "I want to know You." Then allow space in your life for God to speak to you through His Spirit. When you study the Bible, imagine it was written just for you. Study the way God acts in Scripture. Get to know His characteristics. Look for the many different ways God shows love to His people.

God's love is eternal. It doesn't go away when you turn your back on God. It doesn't fluctuate according to your love for Him. It is a constant, abiding love.

God's love is always near, and it includes a promise for those who love Him—the promise of everlasting life.

I Will

Know that God's love is beyond compare.   *yes*   *no*

Understand that God's love prompted Him to send
Jesus to die for my sins.   *yes*   *no*

Be thankful that God loved me enough to give me
a new chance to know Him.   *yes*   *no*

Recognize that God's love is a personal love.   *yes*   *no*

Realize that God's love is eternal.   *yes*   *no*

Accept that God's love will always be near.   *yes*   *no*

Look for ways to express my gratitude for God's
love.   *yes*   *no*

Things to Do

☐ *Thank God for loving you enough to sacrifice His son and build a bridge back to God.*

☐ *Write a poem describing how you feel about God's love.*

☐ *Make a list of human characteristics of love and then compare these to your understanding of God's love.*

☐ *Look at a book on astronomy and attempt to grasp the "bigness" of the universe. Then consider what it means that God's love is more amazing than the size of the universe.*

☐ *Talk with a Christian friend about how you can show thanks to God for His love.*

☐ *Sing along with a gospel CD praising God's great love.*

Things to Remember

He who does not love does not know God, for God is love.

> 1 JOHN 4:8 NKJV

We know how much God loves us, and we have put our trust in Him. God is love, and all who live in love live in God, and God lives in them.

> 1 JOHN 4:16 NKJV

The LORD has appeared of old to me, saying: "Yes, I have loved you with an everlasting love; therefore with lovingkindness I have drawn you."

> JEREMIAH 31:3 NKJV

Hope does not disappoint, because the love of God has been poured out in our hearts by the Holy Spirit who was given to us.

> ROMANS 5:5 NKJV

May the Lord direct your hearts into the love of God and into the patience of Christ.

> 2 THESSALONIANS 3:5 NKJV

God our Savior showed us his kindness and love.

> TITUS 3:4 NLT

God does not love us because we are valuable. We are valuable because God loves us.

—FULTON J. SHEEN

If God takes your lump of clay and remolds it, it will be on the basis of love and not on the basis of power over you.

—JAMES CONWAY

Selfishness

It's All About Me

Let nothing be done through selfish ambition or conceit, but in lowliness of mind let each esteem others better than himself.
—*Philippians 2:3* NKJV

You are living in the me generation. But unlike many other generations, this one has actually been going on for thousands of years. Beginning with the first time someone said "Hey, that's mine! Give it back," the driving philosophy of this generation has been: "It's all about me."

Today, that philosophy informs the lifestyle of millions of people across the globe, though it seems particularly popular with Americans. From the young, who say in word and deed, "I am the center of the known universe," to the not-so-young, who put their personal interests ahead of all others, this approach to life has become commonplace.

Paul, in his letter to the Philippians, reduces this philosophy of life to rubble with a pronouncement that it is better to seek the good of others than to take care of number one. Selfishness is like a virus that has spread through advertisements, through the corporate world, and even through contact with other people. However Paul's caution to the Philippians reaches across time to today. "Don't think only of yourself," he might say. "Instead, give of your time, talent, and even money to help others."

Being thankful for all you have right now can help fight off the selfishness virus. Look around at everything you have. Without comparing your things with those that others have, humbly consider all the gifts God has given you.

Stop buying into the world's philosophy of success. According to the world, the person who dies with the most stuff wins the race of life. God says no, that's not it. Success in God's eyes is all about how you live in relationship to Him and to others. Do you love others? Serve others? Give sacrificially to others? That's what makes you successful in God's eyes. Rediscover the value of relationships.

Consider the needs of others. Each person you run into in any given day is dealing with the trails of life just as you are. You are not the only one who has a difficult job, a troublesome relative, or a car that doesn't start on cold mornings. Invest yourself in the lives of others. Ask them how they're doing. Reduce the number of "I" messages and spend more time listening. Look for ways to help others through life's challenges, and your own life will be enriched in ways that selfish pursuits could never match.

I Will

Know that God desires me to be unselfish.   *yes*   *no*

Realize that selfishness is a driving motivation for
many people's lives.   *yes*   *no*

Examine what it means to give unselfishly to others.   *yes*   *no*

Accept that I will have to wrestle with selfish
desires from time to time.   *yes*   *no*

Endeavor to ignore the world's philosophy that more
is better.   *yes*   *no*

Consider the needs of others.   *yes*   *no*

Look for self-worth in relationships rather than in
possessions.   *yes*   *no*

Things to Do

☐ Ask God to give you a heart of generosity.

☐ Read Acts 4:34–35 and come up with one practical way you might
apply the message of this passage in your own life.

☐ Evaluate your selfishness quotient from one (not at all selfish) to ten
(extremely selfish). Determine one way to lower that number.

☐ Fill a box with items you can do without (not just things you don't
want) and donate them to a local charity or church family.

☐ Ask a close friend to evaluate your generosity.

☐ Review your calendar and determine one way you can change things so
you give more time to others.

Things to Remember

Let no one seek his own, but each one the other's well-being.

1 CORINTHIANS 10:24 NKJV

Love your enemies, do good, and lend, hoping for nothing in return; and your reward will be great, and you will be sons of the Most High. For He is kind to the unthankful and evil.

LUKE 6:35 NKJV

All seek their own, not the things which are of Christ Jesus.

PHILIPPIANS 2:21 NKJV

If a brother or sister is naked and destitute of daily food, and one of you says to them, "Depart in peace, be warmed and filled," but you do not give them the things which are needed for the body, what does it profit?

JAMES 2:15–16 NKJV

Be kindly affectionate to one another with brotherly love, in honor giving preference to one another.

ROMANS 12:10 NKJV

I find life an exciting business, and most exciting when it is lived for others.

—HELEN KELLER

Lord, grant that I may seek to comfort rather than be comforted.

—MOTHER TERESA

Setting and Reaching Goals

Press On

Not that I have already attained, or am already perfected; but I press on, that I may lay hold of that for which Christ Jesus has also laid hold of me.

—Philippians 3:12 NKJV

It is not uncommon for college students to flail and fumble around during their first year or two of school. Eventually, most find their footing, but only after they have locked in on a specific goal. The same is true in many other areas of life. Consider a garage that needs cleaning. You could walk by the clutter a hundred times without making a dent in it. But until you turn a nebulous *This garage is messy* thought into a goal—*I'm going to clean the garage this Saturday*—the mess will likely remain.

Some goals, like cleaning a garage or choosing a career path, have a sense of finality to them. Once the goal is met, it's gone and it's time to choose another one Other goals, like the goal of having a perfect faith, are lifelong pursuits.

When you set goals, know that getting there may require perseverance. Paul's determination to press on toward his goal is a great example of this. Goals such as graduating from school, getting a promotion at work, and sending grown children off into the world can be written on a calendar, but they still require daily steps to accomplish. Broader goals, such as growing in your relationship with God and with other people, may have milestones along the way, but will only move forward if you keep on trying.

Paul's goal was clearly anchored in his relationship with God, but that doesn't mean God alone should be in your lifetime goal. Think about career goals, family goals, and relationship goals you have. Is God in these goals? Consider how your faith affects the structure and purpose of your goals. For example, a goal to get a new job might also include space for trusting God to lead you to the right job, regular prayer time asking God for direction, and willingness to go wherever God might lead, even if it's in a different direction from what you might have hoped for.

Paul's goal was realistic in the sense that he didn't claim he would find closure in this lifetime. Your goals ought to be realistic and reachable too. If the goal is, like Paul's, one that lasts a lifetime, don't expect to make it in a year or two. Know that your goal will always be before you, and stay focused on the target. If your goal is related to your career, set a timetable that makes sense based on your current position. If your goal is relational, plan the steps you must take to reach the goal.

Setting mini goals, or reachable steps, along the way toward a bigger goal is a great way to keep your feet moving in the right direction. It's admirable to have a goal that says "I want to make a difference in the world." What steps will you take to get there? Can you do this in your current life situation? What changes must be made along the way? Look at your bigger goals (and even medium-sized ones) and divide them into smaller pieces. Each little accomplishment along the way will provide the stimulus to keep on going.

Be prepared for both subtle direction changes and abrupt turns along the road to your goals. Over time, you and your goals will change. Don't feel bad if your goal of becoming a successful singer, actor, businessperson, or athlete suddenly seems unreachable. Regroup and consider what new goals you might reach for. Perhaps your singing talent can make a difference in the lives of others at church. Maybe you can use your acting experience in a teaching job or your business experience in a company of your own. Don't let the reality of unreached goals dampen your spirits or keep you from setting new ones.

When you do meet a goal—or see progress along the path to your goal—celebrate. Enjoy how far you've come. Soak up the good feelings that accompany accomplishment. Use the momentum you've created to inspire new goals or the new energy you've generated to reach your current goals.

Always seek God's will as you pursue life goals. Ask God for clear direction when the road is foggy. Ask for encouragement when the trail is rocky. And know that God will be there when you make a wrong turn.

Do you not know that those who run in a race all run, but one receives the prize? Run in such a way that you may obtain it.
—1 Corinthians 9:24 NKJV

I Will

Consider where God fits in my goals.   _yes_   _no_

Know that it is good to set goals in life.   _yes_   _no_

Realize some goals will be lifelong pursuits.   _yes_   _no_

Learn to persevere in order to reach goals.   _yes_   _no_

Set realistic goals.   _yes_   _no_

Recognize that sometimes goals change.   _yes_   _no_

Celebrate successful completion of goals or of steps
toward goals.   _yes_   _no_

Things to Do

☐ *Ask God to give you clear direction on a goal you're trying to reach.*

☐ *List a lifelong goal you have and some of the steps you've already taken toward accomplishing that goal.*

☐ *Write down one goal you have yet to accomplish and what obstacles you face as you attempt to reach that goal.*

☐ *Invite a friend to lunch. Talk together about the goals you have in relation to friends, family, career, and faith.*

☐ *Read a book on goal-setting.*

☐ *Write on your calendar, steps you can take toward accomplishing a goal that has closure (such as cleaning the house, putting in a garden, completing a degree or course at school, and so on).*

Things to Remember

Songs of joy and victory are sung in the camp of the godly.

PSALM 118:15 NLT

All athletes practice strict self-control. They do it to win a prize that will fade away, but we do it for an eternal prize.

1 CORINTHIANS 9:25 NKJV

God never changes his mind about the people he calls and the things he gives them.

ROMANS 11:29 NCV

Do not boast about tomorrow, for you do not know what a day may bring forth.
—Proverbs 27:1 NKJV

Then we will no longer be infants, tossed back and forth by the waves, and blown here and there by every wind of teaching and by the cunning and craftiness of men in their deceitful scheming.

EPHESIANS 4:14 NIV

Jesus said, "When He, the Spirit of truth, has come, He will guide you into all truth; for He will not speak on His own authority, but whatever He hears He will speak; and He will tell you things to come."

JOHN 16:13 NKJV

When Christ returns, I will be proud that I did not lose the race and that my work was not useless.

PHILIPIANS 2:16 NLT

Seek his will in all you do, and he will direct your paths.

PROVERBS 3:6 NLT

Paul wrote: I run straight to the goal with purpose in every step. I am not like a boxer who misses his punches.

1 CORINTHIANS 9:26 NLT

Look what happens to mighty warriors who do not trust in God. They trust their wealth instead and grow more and more bold in their wickedness.

PSALM 52:7 NKJV

Work hard to prove that you really are among those God has called and chosen, and then you will never stumble or fall away.

2 PETER 1:10 TLB

The only light upon the future is faith.

—THEODOR HOECKER

Do not despise your situation. In it you must act, suffer and conquer. From every point on earth, we are equally near to heaven and the infinite.

—HENRI FRÉDÉRIC AMIEL

Eternal Life

Out of Time

This is the promise that He has promised us—eternal life.

—1 John 2:25 NKJV

Do a Web search on the word *eternal* and you'll come up with more than a million hits, referencing everything from the song "Eternal Flame" by the Bangles to vampires to video games, along with a multitude of religious and quasi-religious sites. The same word is used casually in advertising too. Wouldn't you like to enjoy eternal youth simply by applying some fancy cream from a little jar?

The concept of *eternity* comes, of course, from the only person who's known what it looks like: God. It is a word that literally means "for all time." But despite the fact that eternal life is God's alone to give, people continue to search for a way to hang on to one more day of life on earth through health, mysticism, and even religion.

God has said quite plainly that you can't do a thing to add to your days here on earth (Psalm 39:4). They are numbered. However, He also promises the brass ring of eternity for all who follow Him. The fountain of youth may be fiction, but the possibility of living forever is not.

How can you get a handle on something that is so far beyond earthly, time-bound understanding? You can't, at least not fully. But you can know that eternal life is a promise.

It is possible to get so caught up by the promise of eternal life that today might seem almost meaningless. But that's not the point of God's promise. Eternal life is a gift for those who follow God, but it isn't something to rush off to. God desires that you first live your life fully on earth. Get to know God today. Delve into God's Word and seek understanding of God's will. Then, when your days are up, you get the prize of eternal life.

You may be wondering what eternal life might look like. Though the Bible's depiction of heaven includes clues to life after death, the human mind simply can't paint a clear picture of "forever."

You can enjoy the hope of eternity today. That hope can fuel those difficult days you're going to experience while still on earth. It can diminish the pain and suffering you experience by helping you see an eternal perspective. And it can motivate you to make choices that will matter in eternity—focusing on making a difference in the lives of others instead of storing up worldly goods.

I Will

Realize that eternity is something only God fully
understands.

yes no

Know that I can't add a day to my life here on
earth.

yes no

Understand that the promise of eternal life is for
those who follow God.

yes no

Be thankful for the gift of eternal life.

yes no

Not focus on eternity so much that I forget to live
my life today.

yes no

Recognize that I can't paint an accurate picture of
eternal life.

yes no

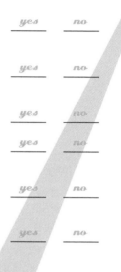

Things to Do

☐ Ask God to reveal how the hope of eternal life ought to influence your
daily decisions.

☐ Interview five or ten children in a Sunday school class about what
eternal life means to them and then compare their answers to your
beliefs on eternal life.

☐ Do your own Web search on the word eternal. See what you can learn
about what people believe lasts forever.

☐ Make a list of actions that have a positive eternal significance and
choose to do some of these.

☐ Draw or paint an abstract picture representing your feelings about
eternal life.

Things to Remember

A certain ruler asked Him, saying, "Good Teacher, what shall I do to inherit eternal life?"

LUKE 18:18 NKJV

Many of those who sleep in the dust of the earth shall awake, some to everlasting life, some to shame and everlasting contempt.

DANIEL 12:2 NKJV

Jesus said, "No one who drinks the water I give will ever be thirsty again. The water I give is like a flowing fountain that gives eternal life."

JOHN 4:14 CEV

Jesus said, "This is the way to have eternal life—to know you, the only true God, and Jesus Christ, the one you sent to earth."

JOHN 17:3 NLT

He will give eternal life to those who patiently do the will of God, seeking for the unseen glory and honor and eternal life that he offers.

ROMANS 2:7 TLB

Here in this world He bids us come, there in the next He shall bid us welcome.

—JOHN DONNE

Surely God would not have created such a being as man . . . to exist only for a day! No, no, man was made for immortality.

—ABRAHAM LINCOLN

Trust

Essential

So shall I have an answer for him who reproaches me, for I trust in Your word.

—*Psalm 119:42 NKJV*

When you bring up the subject of trust, some people immediately bristle. Silent sirens go off and protective walls go up. Past experience with the betrayal of trust has taught these people well: "Don't trust anyone," they say.

There are times when trust is relatively undemanding. Every time you step onto an airplane, bus, or train, you trust that the pilot, driver, or engineer knows what he or she is doing. If you've ever eaten at a restaurant, you've practiced trust. If you've ever stepped into an elevator, you've practiced trust.

But there is more to trust than counting on the fact that others believe in the sanctity of life as much you do. Could you really live your life to its fullest potential if you couldn't trust your friends or family members? Probably not. You'd spend far too much time being paranoid, worrying about the next encounter and whether or not you were being told the truth.

No one ever said learning to trust is easy. But the Bible

says it is a worthy goal. And while it is desirable to learn to trust other people within appropriate limits, it is essential to learn to trust God. Trust brings growth in a relationship. Trust brings you closer to God.

The first step in learning to trust God is to know that God works differently from people. God is perfect, and cares for you and about your life. People, while often earnest in their desire to be trustworthy, sometimes will fail. Imagine the most trusting person you know—God is infinitely more trustworthy. Know that you can count on God and His Word.

Trusting God also means accepting that God always knows what's best for you. When you trust other people, you hope that they have your best interests in mind. Sometimes they do, but sometimes they don't. The hard thing about trusting God is that His definition of what's best for you may not always match what you think is best for you. Trusting God means accepting this potential disparity and allowing God to be right.

Trust is a lot like falling. When you are cautious about trusting others, you may fall with both arms out, ready to brace yourself should no one show up to catch you. But when you fully trust someone, you can fall backward in full confidence that whatever happens, you'll be okay.

I Will

Know that sometimes it's difficult to trust others.   _yes_   _no_

Realize that trusting God is different from trusting
other people.   _yes_   _no_

Recognize that without trust, I can't grow closer to
God.   _yes_   _no_

Know that God is trustworthy.   _yes_   _no_

Believe God knows what's best for me.   _yes_   _no_

Learn to fall backward with confidence that God
will catch me.   _yes_   _no_

Things to Do

- [ ] *Ask God to show you how to trust Him in all areas of life.*

- [ ] *Read Jeremiah 1 and examine Jeremiah's trust relationship with God.*

- [ ] *Invite friends over and take turns going on a trust walk, where one person is blindfolded and led around by others. Debrief this experience.*

- [ ] *List things that make it difficult for you to trust God.*

- [ ] *Recall one time God was there for you. Then consider what this teaches you about trusting God.*

- [ ] *Talk with a trustworthy friend about what it takes to trust other people.*

Things to Remember

Many sorrows shall be to the wicked;
but he who trusts in the LORD, mercy
shall surround him.

PSALM 32:10 NKJV

Our heart shall rejoice in Him, because
we have trusted in His holy name.

PSALM 33:21 NKJV

Let all who take refuge in you be glad;
let them ever sing for joy. Spread your
protection over them, that those who
love your name may rejoice in you.

PSALM 5:11 NIV

I will not trust in my bow, nor shall my
sword save me.

PSALM 44:6 NKJV

This is what the LORD says: "Cursed are
those who put their trust in mere
humans and turn their hearts away from
the Lord."

JEREMIAH 17:5 NKJV

The Scripture says, "Whoever believes on
Him will not be put to shame."

ROMANS 10:11 NKJV

He who trusts in
himself is lost. He
who trusts in God
can do all things.

—SAINT ALPHONSUS
LIGUORI

What is more
elevating and
transporting, than
the generosity of
heart which risks
everything on God's
word?

—JOHN HENRY NEWMAN

Money

Lock-Box Heart

Where your treasure is, there your heart will be also.

—Matthew 6:21 NKJV

It's somewhat ironic that the phrase *In God We Trust* is printed on U.S. currency. For millions of people, the phrase really ought to read *In Money We Trust*. If you were to survey a group of people with the question "What's the one thing you need more of?" your results would include two answers that dominate the rest: time and money. In application, these might end up being the very same answer—remember the phrase *Time is money?*

What is it about money that is so attractive to people? For one, it represents a dubious promise of security. If I have lots of money, people surmise, I won't have any other troubles. The world encourages such thinking by making subtle and obvious claims that wealth will make you happy—that it will solve all your problems. Even though there are hundreds of stories disproving this worldly view (consider the tragic plight of Howard Hughes, for example), people continue to race toward the empty promises of wealth like lemmings heading for the sea.

Money itself isn't evil. Without it you sure would have a difficult time acquiring food, shelter, and clothing. But when money becomes the center of your world, it's not about money anymore—it's about idolatry. Jesus spoke about this many times in Scripture, but never so clearly as when he simply stated, "Wherever your treasure is, there your heart will be also." Whatever it is you treasure most becomes your god. If that thing is money, you have a lock-box heart. Here's why that's a problem: If your god is anything except for the one true God, life is empty and unsatisfying.

Even the wealthiest—and perhaps more significantly, the wisest—man of his time, Solomon, learned this important lesson. Check out Ecclesiastes 5:10 where he states, "He who loves silver will not be satisfied with silver; nor he who loves abundance, with increase. This also is vanity."

Okay, so money isn't bad, but the love of money is. So what's a healthy perspective on money? It begins with the realization that your wealth (whether it is lots or not), really belongs to God. You're just taking care of it while you're on this earth.

Because you're a money manager and not an owner, it's important to learn how to be responsible with money. If you're already under the burden of debt, find someone who can help you dig your way out. Meet with a credit counseling service representative. Make a plan to get out of debt. And whether you're getting out of debt or are now debt-free, stick to a frugal budget that shows restraint and puts God's interests first. Ignore the more-is-better messages that flood the airwaves, and be content with what you have today.

Learn how to balance the pursuit of income with the value of relationships. God wants to spend time with you. God also wants you to spend time with your family and friends. If your pursuit of riches steals too much of that time, you're allowing money to become your God. Budget your time as well as your money.

Admit your weaknesses. Are you an early-adopter when it comes to technology? Do you have to have the latest fashions in order to feel good about yourself? Realize what it is that tempts you to spend unwisely, and stay away from that thing. Consider choosing a friend who can be an accountability partner for you. Pray for strength to fight the temptations to spend unwisely.

If you're having a tough time making ends meet, it could be time to cut back on expenses. Can you do without cable TV for a while? How about changing from brand-name to store-brand clothing or food? Perhaps it's time to consider a different job (just don't choose one that will eat up all of your relationship time). If you're making a comfortable living, look for ways to help others. Give generously to church and charities alike. There's no need to feel guilty if you're making good money unless you hoard it. Be thankful for your good fortune, and share it with others.

The love of money can lead to relational ruin. But wise management of money—and a heart that's focused on God— can make a positive difference in your life and the lives of those you love.

I Will

Attempt to live as if I am merely managing God's money.

yes _____ *no* _____

Understand that if money is my treasure, then God is relegated to second place at best.

yes _____ *no* _____

Know that the love of money is a dangerous thing.

yes _____ *no* _____

Recognize that money is necessary in today's society.

yes _____ *no* _____

Realize that if I make the pursuit of money too important, relationships will suffer.

yes _____ *no* _____

Review my budget and reduce debt if necessary.

yes _____ *no* _____

Things to Do

☐ *Ask God to give you a healthy perspective on money.*

☐ *Fold a dollar bill so the words In God We Trust are displayed prominently. Tape this bill to your bathroom mirror or some other place to remind you where you should put your trust.*

☐ *Look up the word money in a Bible concordance and read the associated Scripture passages.*

☐ *Review your current budget and make adjustments as necessary to reduce debt or increase giving.*

☐ *Talk with a credit counselor if you have serious debt issues.*

☐ *Calculate the average number of hours you've worked in recent weeks. If they seem excessive, come up with two or three ideas for reducing them.*

Things to Remember

The love of money is a root of all kinds of evil, for which some have strayed from the faith in their greediness, and pierced themselves through with many sorrows.

1 TIMOTHY 6:10 NKJV

In the Parable of the Talents, Jesus said, "So you ought to have deposited my money with the bankers, and at my coming I would have received back my own with interest."

MATTHEW 25:27 NKJV

> *Jesus said, "Wherever your treasure is, there your heart and thoughts will also be."*
> —Luke 12:34 TLB

You shall truly tithe all the increase of your grain that the field produces year by year.

DEUTERONOMY 14:22 NKJV

Jesus said to him, "If you wish to be perfect, go, sell your possessions, and give the money to the poor, and you will have treasure in heaven; then come, follow me."

MATTHEW 19:21 NRSV

Do not lay up for yourselves treasures on earth, where moth and rust destroy and where thieves break in and steal.

MATTHEW 6:19 NKJV

My God shall supply all your need according to His riches in glory by Christ Jesus.

PHILIPPIANS 4:19 NKJV

Jesus said, "Lay up for yourselves treasures in heaven, where neither moth nor rust destroys and where thieves do not break in and steal."

MATTHEW 6:20 NKJV

Really! There's no such thing as self-rescue, pulling yourself up by your bootstraps. The cost of rescue is beyond our means.

PSALM 49:6 THE MESSAGE

Jesus said, "He who is faithful in what is least is faithful also in much; and he who is unjust in what is least is unjust also in much."

LUKE 16:10 NKJV

Will you set your eyes on that which is not? For riches certainly make themselves wings; they fly away like an eagle toward heaven.

PROVERBS 23:5 NKJV

Getting riches brings care; keeping them brings trouble; abusing them brings guilt; and losing them brings sorrow. It is a great mistake to make so much of riches as we do.

—D. L. MOODY

If you make money your god, it will plague you like the devil.

—HENRY FIELDING

Solitude

Even in the Quietest Moments

After he had dismissed them, he went up on a mountainside by himself to pray. When evening came, he was there alone.

—*Matthew 14:23* NIV

Do you ever wish you could just snap your fingers and be whisked away from the rattle and thunder of a busy day? Have you ever wondered what a moment in life would sound like apart from the chatter, the clatter, and the commotion of friends, family, coworkers, and neighbors? Silence is a precious commodity in a noise-marinated world.

It seems that everyone longs for silence and time alone, for peace and quiet. But silence isn't always so easy to find. At times, it may seem impossible. Even in the cacophony, however, you can find solitude. Solitude is taking time away from the push and pull of the day—it's a deliberate time dedicated to your needs.

Even Jesus needed solitude. According to Matthew, immediately after Jesus had fed five thousand people, He sent His disciples across the lake and headed up a mountainside. Alone. Away from the murmur of the crowd. Away even from the familiar voices of his closest friends.

Finding solitude isn't always unproblematic. You may not be able to physically get away from the noise. But you can learn to focus inwardly for a time—to blot out the distractions and enter a time of quiet. The key to doing this well is accepting the fact that you don't need to know everything that's going on around you all of the time.

If you have the freedom to select a regular time for solitude, do it. If you're a morning person, get up extra early and enjoy your time while others in the household are asleep. If you're a late-riser, consider staying up a little longer each day for that time alone. If you can't choose a regular time, learn to seize the moment when it comes. Grab time alone when a lunch meeting is cancelled at the last minute, or when a bus or train is delayed. Rather than stress out about the change to your schedule, enjoy your extra God-supplied moments for time alone with Him. Be deliberate about taking time to be alone with God.

When you're alone with God, listen. Allow the silence to be God's time for speaking to you. Perhaps the quiet itself will be God's message to you. Maybe God will nudge you toward change. Or perhaps you will simply be comforted to know God loves you. Expect to meet God when you are alone, and He will be there.

I Will

Expect to encounter God in my solitude.

yes _____ _no_ _____

Drink in God's comfort and love when I'm alone.

yes _____ _no_ _____

Be deliberate about taking time to be alone with God.

yes _____ _no_ _____

Seek times of solitude even when quiet isn't possible.

yes _____ _no_ _____

Acknowledge that moments of solitude are important in my life.

yes _____ _no_ _____

Endeavor to be more confident and patient in the workaday world, knowing that time alone with God awaits.

yes _____ _no_ _____

Things to Do

☐ *Ask God to always meet you in your quiet times.*

☐ *Read Psalm 62.*

☐ *Turn off everything that's making a sound and spend five minutes by yourself in the quiet.*

☐ *Choose a location at home or at work where you can regularly go to be by yourself for a time.*

☐ *Ask a friend or family member to hold you accountable in your desire to make time for solitude.*

☐ *If you live in a safe neighborhood, go outside late at night when the world's asleep and listen to the sound of solitude. (Or simply open a window and listen.)*

Things to Remember

Jesus said, "Come to me, all of you who are tired and have heavy loads, and I will give you rest."

MATTHEW 11:28 NCV

I wait quietly before God, for my salvation comes from him. He alone is my rock and my salvation, my fortress where I will never be shaken.

PSALM 62:1–2 NLT

Anyone who enters God's rest also rests from his own work, just as God did from his.

HEBREWS 4:10 NIV

Jehovah is my refuge! I choose the God above all gods to shelter me.

PSALM 91:9 TLB

The apostles gathered around Jesus, and told him all that they had done and taught. He said to them, "Come away to a deserted place all by yourselves and rest a while."

MARK 6:30–31 NRSV

Jesus said, "When you pray, go into your room, and when you have shut your door, pray to your Father who is in the secret place; and your Father who sees in secret will reward you openly."

MATTHEW 6:6 NKJV

A solitude is the audience-chamber of God.

—WALTER SAVAGE LANDOR

I never found the companion that was so companionable as solitude.

—HENRY DAVID THOREAU

Sexuality

The Original Plan

Flee sexual immorality. Every sin that a man does is outside the body, but he who commits sexual immorality sins against his own body.

—*1 Corinthians 6:18 NKJV*

It's nearly impossible to ignore the world's fascination with sex. The sex-sells philosophy drives television, music, and movies. Some so-called experts hail this new era as a healthy time for sexuality. But the world's view on sex is a mishmash of lies, empty promises, and misinformation.

Read God's Word to discover the true purpose and place of sex. Genesis tells of the creation of sex and its most significant purpose—to multiply humanity. However, God also added a condition to sex: that it be reserved solely for those who are committed to each other through marriage.

Sexual immorality began soon after the fall. It's not something new to this century. Many of Paul's letters included specific cautions about sex. In the days of the early church, pagan religions flourished—many of them promoting sexual experimentation and "freedom." Though the landscape has changed, the issues remain much the same. Paul's cautions are just as valid today and say quite simply, Don't toy with God's original plan for sex.

Paul also reminded Christians to avoid sexual temptation. In a world where even TV commercials scream out Sex for sale! that can be a real challenge. But it is possible. You can turn off the TV and use your time for reading instead. Or make more careful choices about what shows you watch. Since ratings and reviews often include reference to sexual content, read multiple reviews of movies before you go. Limit your online time at the computer. If inappropriate Internet content tempts you, have a trusted friend install a filter or simply hold you accountable to your online activities. Evaluate any potentially compromising positions you might face with coworkers, friends, or acquaintances. Avoid situations that would place you alone with someone of the opposite sex who isn't your spouse (such as business lunches, work trips, and so on).

It would be unfortunate and incomplete to explore sexuality without discussing the second reason God created it: to be enjoyed! A thorough reading of the Song of Solomon should clarify any questions about how much God wanted people to enjoy sex. Once again, however, sex is placed squarely in the context of marriage.

To understand the role of sex for your life, forget what the world teaches and go to the original source. Go to God. He wants your experience with sex to be fulfilling and complete—and He knows that can only truly happen in the context of marriage.

I Will

Understand that the Bible has a lot to say about sex.   *yes*   *no*

Recognize that one purpose of sex is procreation.   *yes*   *no*

Know that God created sex to be enjoyed by married couples.   *yes*   *no*

Realize that God's original plan for sex is still valid today.   *yes*   *no*

Know that the world's view of sex is all messed up.   *yes*   *no*

Be aware that it's difficult to avoid the philosophy of sex or sexuality presented by the world.   *yes*   *no*

Look for ways to avoid sexual temptation.   *yes*   *no*

Things to Do

☐ *Thank God for the gift of sexuality and its proper place in the context of marriage.*

☐ *Read the Song of Solomon.*

☐ *With your spouse or some good friends, watch a popular television show and then discuss how the show's view on sex compares with God's plan.*

☐ *Determine one or two things you can do to reduce the influence of the world's view of sex in your life.*

☐ *Skim the contents of a favorite mainstream magazine and tally the number of ads or articles that use sex to sell.*

☐ *Study what Paul has to say about purity in 1 Thessalonians 4:1–8.*

Things to Remember

God created man in His own image; in the image of God He created him; male and female He created them.

GENESIS 1:27 NKJV

Be happy, yes, rejoice in the wife of your youth. Let her breasts and tender embrace satisfy you. Let her love alone fill you with delight.

PROVERBS 5:18–19 TLB

A man shall leave his father and mother and be joined to his wife, and they shall become one flesh.

GENESIS 2:24 NKJV

Let him kiss me with the kisses of his mouth—for your love is better than wine.

SONG OF SOLOMON 1:2 NKJV

Let the husband render to his wife the affection due her, and likewise also the wife to her husband.

1 CORINTHIANS 7:3 NKJV

You shall not commit adultery.

EXODUS 20:14 NKJV

Love may or may not include sexual attraction. It may express itself in sexual desire. But sexual desire is not love. Desire is quite compatible with personal hatred, or contempt, or indifference.

—JOHN MACMURRAY

Sexuality throws no light upon love, but only through love can we learn to understand sexuality.

—EUGEN ROSENSTOCK-HUESSY

Self-Esteem

Knitting Pattern

Before I formed you in the womb I knew you; before you were born I sanctified you; I ordained you a prophet to the nations.

—*Jeremiah 1:5 NKJV*

Low self-esteem is a uniquely human condition. It is also one of the most universal human experiences. Its symptoms can be quite diverse. For some, low self-esteem manifests itself as a hidden existence defined by sad, quiet loneliness. For others, it results in an outwardly self-assured mask—a life-of-the-party shell that serves only to hide low self-confidence.

The great paradox of low self-esteem is that it's really not about the self at all. It's about others' approval. For many people, the image they have of themselves is only as positive as the messages they've received from others—particularly family members and peers. That explains why a person who seems to have it all may feel far more inferior than someone who has very little. It all depends on the environment, the circumstance, and how much the person believes in the worldly images of success and beauty.

If you have a good self-esteem today, be thankful.

Chances are, you have long given up on trying to make yourself into the world's image of beauty. That's the first step toward building a strong self-esteem. If you look closely at the images of success as painted by the world (particularly by the media—magazines, movies, television), you'll notice they're fantasies. They are unreal, rather than ideal.

The second step toward building positive self-esteem is to realize that your worth shouldn't be solely anchored in relationships with others. If you suffer from chronic low self-esteem, you already know this truth all too well. If you were lucky enough to have been given positive reinforcement early in life, you probably feel fairly self-confident today. But even a strong foundation of confidence isn't always enough to thwart the esteem-toppling power of an uncaring supervisor, a mean-spirited coworker, or even a misguided relative.

The only way to discover self-esteem that won't change with the wind is to realize what Jeremiah discovered—that your true worth is found only in the God who created you. God knew Jeremiah was right for the job of prophet even though Jeremiah was sure he couldn't do it. God knew exactly how He had created Jeremiah and knew what Jeremiah could and couldn't do. Once Jeremiah accepted that God knew him better than he knew himself, he discovered confidence far beyond what the world had given him.

God knows how He created you too. Trust that God knows you better than you know yourself and you will secure your self-image to Him. Self-esteem anchored to God can never be taken away.

I Will

Accept that my true worth is found only in God.　　*yes*　　*no*

Examine what it means to be a unique creation of
God.　　*yes*　　*no*

Trust that God knows me better than I know myself.　　*yes*　　*no*

Realize that it's common to struggle with low self-
esteem.　　*yes*　　*no*

Know that the world's view of beauty or success
isn't the ideal.　　*yes*　　*no*

Recognize the value of positive reinforcement from
parents or friends.　　*yes*　　*no*

Things to Do

☐ *Thank God for loving you just the way you are.*

☐ *Study the life of Jeremiah (particularly chapter 1 and chapters 46–51)
and learn how God used Jeremiah's unique abilities as a prophet.*

☐ *Write a thank-you note to someone who has been a positive influence
in your life.*

☐ *Ask a trusted friend to tell you one or two positive things that make
you unique.*

☐ *Draw a self-portrait according to the way you see yourself. Then draw
one the way God might picture you.*

☐ *Call and encourage a friend who might be suffering from low self-
esteem.*

Things to Remember

I will praise You, for I am fearfully and wonderfully made; marvelous are Your works, and that my soul knows very well.

PSALM 139:14 NKJV

In Him dwells all the fullness of the Godhead bodily; and you are complete in Him, who is the head of all principality and power.

COLOSSIANS 2:9–10 NKJV

God demonstrates His own love toward us, in that while we were still sinners, Christ died for us.

ROMANS 5:8 NKJV

The LORD said to Samuel, "Do not look at his appearance or at the height of his stature, because I have refused him. For the Lord does not see as man sees; for man looks at the outward appearance, but the Lord looks at the heart."

1 SAMUEL 16:7 NKJV

Shall the clay say to him who forms it, "What are you making?" Or shall your handiwork say, "He has no hands"?

ISAIAH 45:9 NKJV

In a world of prayer, we are all equal in the sense that each of us is a unique person, with a unique perspective on the world.

—W. H. AUDEN

No one can make you feel inferior without your consent.

—ELEANOR ROOSEVELT

Finding Your Role in Ministry

Playing Your Part

Just as the body is one and has many members, and all the members of the body, though many, are one body, so it is with Christ.

—*1 Corinthians 12:12* NRSV

At least once a week, pastors all around the world step up to the podium to speak with conviction about faith and life. For some people in the congregation, this is the only picture they get of church. What they may not see each week, however, is the tireless work of the people behind the scenes and in other ministries. A church is much more than a building with a pastor and a pulpit. Paul's sketch of the body of Christ in 1 Corinthians is a perfect description of the church.

While the pastor may be the most prominent "body part," the church could not function without the people who take on other ministry roles. Those roles include everything from property maintenance to food preparation to teaching. And one of those roles may be just right for you.

One of the key factors in determining where you best fit is knowing where your passions lie. Perhaps you have a love for children. Or maybe you love music. Do you have a desire to tell others about God's love? There is likely a ministry opportunity at your church that matches your passion. Narrow your options to those you really think you'd enjoy (children's ministry, evangelism, food pantry, music team, and so forth).

In addition to your passion, it's important to consider your giftedness. In Romans 12, Paul explained that each person who comes to know Christ receives one or more spiritual gifts. A spiritual gift is a God-given talent or ability that can have a positive impact the lives of others. You may already know your gift—or you may not have a clue. If you're not sure what your gift or gifts are, talk with your church pastor. Many churches offer classes or seminars to help you find your giftedness.

Once you know your giftedness and your passion, you should be able to find the perfect place to plug into ministry. Perhaps you have the gift of teaching and a passion for children. Sounds like you'd make a great Sunday school teacher. Or perhaps your gift is mercy and you have a heart for disadvantaged people. Local missions may be a good fit. If at all possible, look for a way to use both your gifts and your passions. Know that when you are in ministry, you are in worship.

I Will

Know that the church is like a body with many
parts.

yes ___ no ___

Consider why I might participate in my local church
ministry.

yes ___ no ___

Understand that all ministry roles are important in
the church.

yes ___ no ___

Examine my areas of passion and how they relate to
ministry opportunities.

yes ___ no ___

Discover my spiritual gifts.

yes ___ no ___

Look for ways to use my giftedness and passions to
help in my church.

yes ___ no ___

Things to Do

☐ *Thank God for the local church and the ways in which He has gifted
you to serve others.*

☐ *If you're already involved in a ministry, contact the ministry director
and thank him or her for allowing you to participate.*

☐ *Attend a class on finding your spiritual gifts or take a spiritual gifts
inventory.*

☐ *Get a copy of your church's organizational chart to learn more about
the ministry opportunities.*

☐ *List three areas of passion and then list ministries these might match
up with.*

Things to Remember

There are diversities of gifts, but the same Spirit.

1 CORINTHIANS 12:4 NKJV

The body is not made up of one part but of many.

1 CORINTHIANS 12:14 NIV

Every good gift and every perfect gift is from above, and comes down from the Father of lights, with whom there is no variation or shadow of turning.

JAMES 1:17 NKJV

Even so you, since you are zealous for spiritual gifts, let it be for the edification of the church that you seek to excel.

1 CORINTHIANS 14:12 NKJV

Though I speak with the tongues of men and of angels, but have not love, I have become sounding brass or a clanging cymbal.

1 CORINTHIANS 13:1 NKJV

Having then gifts differing according to the grace that is given to us, let us use them.

ROMANS 12:6 NKJV

Purpose is what gives life meaning.

—C. H. PARKHURST

When I have learned to do the Father's will, I shall have fully realized my vocation on earth.

—CARLO CARRETTO

God's Forgiveness

Just Ask

Jesus prayed, "Forgive us our debts, as we forgive our debtors."
—Matthew 6:12 NKJV

Two friends sit in a room but don't speak. Tom is torn up inside. He said something hurtful to Lily. He didn't mean to cause her pain. But the words spilled out before he could stop them. He has already asked for forgiveness, but Lily is silent. She's not quite ready to forgive. She is upset and needs to be angry for a while. Meanwhile, Tom's sadness grows with every passing minute.

Forgiveness is a simple act with immeasurable significance. When you forgive someone who has hurt you, you give that person another chance to relate to you. Withholding forgiveness builds an unscalable wall. Unfortunately, people have an incredible ability to withhold forgiveness. Like Lily, they want to be angry for a while. It's normal to go through a processing time when someone has hurt you. But when that time drags on beyond the request for forgiveness, the pain mounts and both parties suffer. Imagine if God withheld forgiveness as easily as humans do. Can you picture what your list of unforgiven sins might look like today?

Thankfully, God doesn't look at forgiveness the same way

people do. He doesn't even consider putting up a wall. Instead, He says, "Come to Me and ask, and you'll be forgiven." That's really all there is to it. Just ask.

It's important to note that there are really two separate-but-related aspects to God's forgiveness. When you accept Christ, your sins are forgiven once and for all. This is the global cleansing that comes with becoming a Christian, and it can never be taken away. This forgiveness is what gives you the "keys to the kingdom," brings you back into a relationship with God, and offers you the promise of eternal life.

Even after you become a Christian, however, you're going to make bad choices. The truth is, even though your faith has made you a new creature, you're still a human creature. You're still fallible.

God wants you to grow up in faith and learn to avoid sin. He also wants you to admit when you've done something wrong. The best way to appropriate God's ongoing forgiveness is to ask for it daily when you pray. Whether you can think of a specific sin or not, you can go to God in prayer and ask Him to forgive you.

What do you need forgiveness for? You can probably think of a few things you've done that go against God's will. Start there. Any time you act in a way that is contrary to God's way, you are committing a sin. Without God's forgiveness, that sin mounts up and threatens to crush you. But with forgiveness comes a clean slate and a chance to do things right. Know, however, that there are consequences to sin. You may damage someone else or yourself through your careless actions or words. The scars of sin don't necessarily disappear with forgiveness.

It's good to know you can't use up God's forgiveness. God's forgiveness is unending. Whether you're making tons of bad choices in a difficult life season or are staying close to God and growing in faith daily, God will hear your confession. Whether your sin seems to be small or huge, God can forgive you. While God's ability to continually forgive doesn't give you license to mess up on purpose, it is good to know God is always ready to forgive.

God's forgiveness is also permanent. You can probably still remember the wrong another person did to you even though you've forgiven that person. But God forgives and forgets. Don't get stuck in the past when you've messed up. Ask for forgiveness and move on. God has already forgotten what you did.

Allow God's forgiveness to change you. It's one thing to be forgiven for a wrongdoing, but something else altogether to learn from it. When you ask for forgiveness, ask also for wisdom and strength to avoid the same sin. Search for advice in the Bible as well as in the counsel of Christian friends. Will God still forgive you if you make the same mistake? Sure. But make it your goal to grow and learn from your mistakes.

David said to Nathan, "I have sinned against the Lord." And Nathan said to David, "The Lord also has put away your sin; you shall not die."
—2 Samuel 12:13 NKJV

I Will

Ask for God's forgiveness often when I pray. _yes_ _no_

Be comforted that I can't use up God's forgiveness. _yes_ _no_

Recognize that God also forgets when He forgives. _yes_ _no_

Know that God's forgiveness is available for the asking. _yes_ _no_

Understand that there are two aspects to God's forgiveness. _yes_ _no_

Endeavor to always learn and grow from my mistakes. _yes_ _no_

Things to Do

☐ *Study the life of a well-known Bible character (such as David in 1 and 2 Samuel) and explore the role God's forgiveness played in that person's life.*

☐ *Make a list of sins for which you've already asked God for forgiveness. Then dispose of that paper in a shredder or fireplace.*

☐ *Ask God for forgiveness from recent wrong attitudes or actions.*

☐ *Invite Christian friends over to talk about what it means to accept God's forgiveness.*

☐ *Write a letter to God, expressing your thanks for His forgiveness.*

☐ *Make a poster that says JUST ASK and display it as a reminder of how to obtain God's forgiveness.*

Things to Remember

It is written that the Christ would suffer and rise from the dead on the third day and that a change of hearts and lives and forgiveness of sins would be preached in his name to all nations, starting at Jerusalem.

LUKE 24:46–47 NCV

When deeds of iniquity overwhelm us, you forgive our transgressions.

PSALM 65:3 NRSV

Create in me a clean heart, O God, and renew a steadfast spirit within me.
—Psalm 51:10 NKJV

Jesus said, "This is My blood of the new covenant, which is shed for many for the remission of sins."

MATTHEW 26:28 NKJV

Help us, O God of our salvation, for the glory of Your name; and deliver us, and provide atonement for our sins, for Your name's sake!

PSALM 103:12 NKJV

An angel of the Lord said to Joseph, "She will bring forth a Son, and you shall call His name JESUS, for He will save His people from their sins."

MATTHEW 1:21 NKJV

You were dead because of your sins and because your sinful nature was not yet cut away. Then God made you alive with Christ. He forgave all our sins.

COLOSSIANS 2:13 NKJV

Jesus said, "If you do not forgive, neither will your Father in heaven forgive your trespasses."

MARK 11:26 NKJV

I will be merciful to their unrighteousness, and their sins and their lawless deeds I will remember no more.

HEBREWS 8:12 NKJV

They sinned against me, but I will wash away that sin. They did evil and turned away from me, but I will forgive them.

JEREMIAH 33:8 NCV

It is indeed amazing that in as fundamentally irreligious a culture as ours, the sense of guilt should be so widespread and deeply rooted as it is.

—ERICH FROMM

When I bring my sins to the Lord Jesus He casts them into the depths of the sea— forgiven and forgotten. He also puts up a sign, "No Fishing Allowed!"

—CORRIE TEN BOOM

A Place of Honor

Hear, O kings! Give ear, O princes! I, even I, will sing to the Lord; I will sing praise to the Lord God of Israel.

—Judges 5:3 NKJV

The word *worship* has limited secular meaning. A sports fan might "worship" his favorite team, or a fan of a pop group might "worship" the ground the lead singer walks on. But that's about it. Usually, when you hear the word *worship*, it's attached to some kind of religious discussion.

People have been worshiping for centuries. Thousands of years ago, people worshiped idols, unseen gods or goddesses, nature, animals, and just about anything else. Some also worshiped the one true God, the God of Israel. Today there are people who still worship everything under the sun, and perhaps even the sun as well. However, mainstream religions have eclipsed the earlier pagan practices, and the number of people who worship anything other than a well-recognized "supreme being" is rather small.

But whether a person worships God or a toadstool, the components of worship are much the same. Worship, at its very core, is "giving high honor" to someone or something. The worshiper also usually accepts that the object of his or her worship has extraordinary power or significance. With one important exception, the relationship between worshiper and the object of worship is strictly one-way. The exception? Christianity.

Since Christian faith is based on a relationship with God, there is a two-way street between the worshiper and the object of worship, God. You can just as easily talk with God as show Him honor. This closeness adds a personal dimension to worship. Far more than ritual, worship for those who are in relationship with God is a uniquely private and meaningful experience.

Worship can happen in many different ways and in many different settings. The most common setting for worship is at church. Communal worship experiences can run the gamut from serious and reverential to emotional and expressive, depending on the church tradition. If the shared experience of worship at church is important to you, be sure to choose a church where you're comfortable with the style.

When you serve others at church, whether in the nursery, as a teacher or as a greeter, you are experiencing a different form of worship. By serving others, you also serve God. This form of worship often results in a sense of satisfaction and joy rather than the emotional high that corporate worship might bring, but it just as valid. God is praised when His people humbly serve one another.

You can also worship in a small-group setting with your family or friends. An informal time of prayer or singing can often be some of the most meaningful worship because of its intimacy. If you aren't already a member of a small group or a study group, consider joining one.

Some of the best worship times will happen when you're alone with God. If you've had your breath taken watching a sunrise across a perfectly still lake, you've probably participated in a form of worship. There is something transcendently awesome about God's creation that can pull you into worship without warning. Perhaps for you it's a sunset or the smell of rain. Those moments are precious and wonderful. Go ahead and seek them out—look for places and times when you can be alone with God enjoying the beauty of creation.

Each time you go to God in prayer—whether it's a formal time of prayer or an informal one—you can also enter a time of worship. Make it a point always to express your love for God and for who He is when you pray. Honor Him with your words and thoughts throughout each day.

There will be times when you don't feel like worshiping. Perhaps you aren't happy with the direction God is leading you. Maybe you're in the middle of a difficult season at work or home. It's important to worship regardless, because worship can help you reconnect with God, and God can offer you solutions to your tough times. Force yourself to go to a worship service. Play praise and worship music at home. Do something that can help you focus on God's awesomeness. Though worship is a God-focused time, you also receive benefit from it—peace, focus, self-worth. A time of worship might be just the thing you need to get out of your funk and refocus on what's important.

I Will

Realize that God is honored when I worship Him.   _yes_   _no_

Recognize that serving others can be a form of
worship.   _yes_   _no_

Know that worship is giving honor.   _yes_   _no_

Understand that worship can happen in many
different ways.   _yes_   _no_

Look for ways to participate in corporate worship.   _yes_   _no_

Enjoy worshiping God in His Creation.   _yes_   _no_

Things to Do

☐ Go to God in prayer and thank Him for who He is.

☐ Determine one way you can worship God by serving others and make a
commitment to do this (put it on your calendar).

☐ Read passages in Scripture that honor God (such as Psalm 150).

☐ Attend an evening worship service.

☐ Write a poem of worship describing reasons God is worthy of honor.

☐ Invite friends to your home for a time of worship singing.

☐ Go to a park, a wilderness area or simply sit outside at night observing
the sky. Use this time to worship God for His incredible creation.

Things to Remember

It will be said in that day: "Behold, this is our God; we have waited for Him, and He will save us. This is the LORD; we have waited for Him; we will be glad and rejoice in His salvation."

ISAIAH 25:9 NKJV

The one thing I want from God, the thing I seek most of all, is the privilege of meditating in his Temple, living in his presence every day of my life, delighting in his incomparable perfections and glory.

PSALM 27:4 TLB

Make a joyful shout to the LORD, all you lands! Serve the LORD with gladness; come before His presence with singing.
—Psalm 100:1–2 NKJV

Moses and Aaron went in and told Pharaoh, "Thus says the LORD God of Israel: 'Let My people go, that they may hold a feast to Me in the wilderness.'"

EXODUS 5:1 NKJV

Praise the LORD! Sing to the LORD a new song, and His praise in the assembly of saints.

PSALM 149:1 NKJV

The LORD said, "You shall have no other gods before Me."

EXODUS 20:3 NKJV

Jesus said, "God is Spirit, and those who worship him must worship in spirit and truth."

JOHN 4:24 CEV

Jesus answered and said to him, "Get behind Me, Satan! For it is written, 'You shall worship the LORD your God, and Him only you shall serve.'"

LUKE 4:8 NKJV

God, who made the world and everything in it, since He is Lord of heaven and earth, does not dwell in temples made with hands.

ACTS 17:24 NKJV

"Go up to the mountains and bring wood and build the temple, that I may take pleasure in it and be glorified," says the LORD.

HAGGAI 1:8 NKJV

Jesus said, "The hour is coming, and now is, when the true worshipers will worship the Father in spirit and truth; for the Father is seeking such to worship Him."

JOHN 4:23 NKJV

Christian worship is the most momentous, the most urgent, the most glorious action that can take place in human life.

—KARL BARTH

The world can be saved by one thing, and that is worship. For to worship is to quicken the conscience by the holiness of God, to feed the mind with the truth of God, to purge the imagination by the beauty of God, to open the heart to the love of God, to devote the will to the purpose of God.

—WILLIAM TEMPLE

Mysterious Ways

Oh, the depth of the riches both of the wisdom and knowledge of God! How unsearchable are His judgments and His ways past finding out!

—*Romans 11:33 NKJV*

People are fascinated by mystery. A quick flip through the local TV listings is proof enough of that. You'll find everything from traditional whodunits to more obscure fare such as shows exploring the possibility of aliens or examining the latest conspiracy theories. The lure of the unknown is strong. People are drawn to mystery in part because they want to solve it, but equally because they want to know there is no plausible answer.

Attempting to comprehend God is like trying to get the answers to all your other mystery questions at the same time. Who else but the only Person who has lived for eternity would understand infinity? Who else but the One who created the universe would know how big it is?

With the limitations of a human mind, you can't fully understand God. Paul was intimately aware of this when he wrote about the depth of God's wisdom in Romans. But that didn't stop Paul from trying to know God. And that is precisely what God desires for you—that you get to know Him.

Because God is relational, you can get to know Him simply by talking with Him. Your knowledge of God will grow according to how much time you spend with Him in prayer. As you learn how God answers prayer, you'll come to know His thoughts. You'll learn what is important to God. And you'll discover that God's ways are not always knowable.

You can also know God by observing His Creation. By studying the stars you can see His greatness, by watching an elephant, His creativity. His greatest creation, people, can teach you much about God—keep in mind that people were created in God's image. Like you, God desires companionship (that is why He created people in the first place). Like you, God desires to be loved without condition (that is why He gave you free will).

Perhaps the best way to know God is to read His résumé: the Bible. Through the stories and wisdom presented in God's Word, you can learn about God's unending love. You can uncover insights into God's character—that He is merciful, just, patient, powerful, all-knowing. There is no end to the amount of truth you can uncover about God by reading the Bible.

Be compelled by the mystery of God to seek Him even more diligently.

I Will

Recognize that God is a God of mystery.   *yes*   *no*

Realize that God wants me to know Him.   *yes*   *no*

Accept that I can't fully know God.   *yes*   *no*

Get to know God through regular prayer.   *yes*   *no*

See God in His creation—particularly through
relationships with other people.   *yes*   *no*

Read the Bible often to better know God.   *yes*   *no*

Be diligent about getting to know God.   *yes*   *no*

Things to Do

☐ *Determine what you consider to be the three greatest mysteries about God or His creation.*

☐ *Watch a mystery on television and compare the characters' desire to solve the mystery with your desire to understand God.*

☐ *Talk with a friend about what excites you most and frustrates you most about the mystery of God.*

☐ *Use a calendar to schedule your Bible reading times for the next week so you can get to know God better.*

☐ *Write down your thoughts about how the following quotation from Albert Einstein relates to your relationship with God: "The most beautiful experience we can have is the mysterious."*

Things to Remember

Therefore You are great, O Lord GOD. For there is none like You, nor is there any God besides You, according to all that we have heard with our ears.

2 SAMUEL 7:22 NKJV

No one has seen God at any time. The only begotten Son, who is in the bosom of the Father, He has declared Him.

JOHN 1:18 NKJV

God is not a man, that He should lie, nor a son of man, that He should repent. Has He said, and will He not do? Or has He spoken, and will He not make it good?

NUMBERS 23:19 NKJV

Solomon said, "Will God indeed dwell on the earth? Behold, heaven and the heaven of heavens cannot contain You. How much less this temple which I have built!"

1 KINGS 8:27 NKJV

If our heart condemns us, God is greater than our heart, and knows all things.

1 JOHN 3:20 NKJV

Righteousness and justice are the foundation of Your throne; mercy and truth go before Your face.

PSALM 89:14 NKJV

His center is everywhere, His circumference is nowhere.

—HENRY LAW

As I read the Bible, I seem to find holiness to be His supreme attribute.

—BILLY GRAHAM

Handling Pain

No More Bruises

A voice from heaven said, "God will wipe away every tear from their eyes; there shall be no more death, nor sorrow, nor crying. There shall be no more pain, for the former things have passed away."

—*Revelation 21:4* NKJV

Pain is an immobilizer. When you're in pain, regular life activities are often put on hold. This makes perfect sense, especially if what you're experiencing is significant physical pain. Imagine, for instance, trying to lift heavy objects at your job when you're suffering from debilitating back spasms. There are very good reasons to alter your life schedule when you're in pain. But what about emotional pain?

When someone hurts you emotionally, the injury may not be obvious to others, but the results often are. As with physical pain, emotional pain can also immobilize you. It can bruise you to the point where regular routines become difficult or even impossible. Yet you still need to function in life. How can you deal with the pain?

First, go ahead and feel the hurt, even though it's uncomfortable. Though it may be necessary for decorum's sake to keep your response hidden for a time, always process your pain. Go to a close friend and ask permission to talk about it. Speak with a pastor or a counselor if the situation warrants. Just don't suppress your feelings for too long or they'll turn to bitterness, or, worse, they'll immobilize you even more than they already have.

Next, do a little time travel. Look ahead to the time when the pain will be only a distant memory. Then look even further, to a time when pain will no longer be a part of life: to the promise of heaven.

In his description of heaven, the author of the book of Revelation paints a beautiful picture of God wiping away all your tears and then removing the possibility of pain. This promise offers comfort in two ways. First, it points to the fact that God is aware of the reality of pain in this life and that He recognizes and cares about your pain. Knowing this can give you confidence to approach God through prayer when you're hurting. Second, the promise gives hope that pain won't always be in the human equation. Though this may offer less immediate comfort, it can help you see that God is ultimately on your side.

Finally, talk to God about your pain. Spend time in prayer, asking for wisdom in dealing with the pain. Ask for strength to continue doing life as you work through the hurt. God will be there for you.

I Will

Look forward to the promise a pain-free existence
in heaven.   *yes*   *no*

Recognize that God understands my pain today.   *yes*   *no*

Talk to God when I'm hurting.   *yes*   *no*

Understand that pain can immobilize me.   *yes*   *no*

Process my pain appropriately rather than
suppress it.   *yes*   *no*

Share my feelings with a close friend, pastor, or
counselor.   *yes*   *no*

Know that time will heal the pain.   *yes*   *no*

Things to Do

☐ *Copy five comforting Scriptures (such as Revelation 21:4 or any other listed in this meditation) onto a sheet of paper, reflecting on the message of each one as you write it.*

☐ *Call a friend and arrange to get together and talk about a recent painful experience.*

☐ *Write down what it is you're feeling right now after reading about dealing with pain.*

☐ *Read Revelation 21:1—22:5 and then think of five things you will look forward to about heaven.*

☐ *Listen to a song about a broken relationship (such as "When Will I Be Loved" or "End of the Innocence") or some other painful experience and compare it to your own life.*

Things to Remember

Even we Christians, although we have the Holy Spirit within us as a foretaste of future glory, also groan to be released from pain and suffering.

ROMANS 8:23 TLB

Those who sow in tears shall reap in joy.

PSALM 126:5 NKJV

My bones are pierced in me at night, and my gnawing pains take no rest.

JOB 30:17 NKJV

We give great honor to those who endure under suffering. Job is an example of a man who endured patiently. From his experience we see how the Lord's plan finally ended in good, for he is full of tenderness and mercy.

JAMES 5:11 NKJV

His anger is but for a moment, His favor is for life; weeping may endure for a night, but joy comes in the morning.

PSALM 30:5 NKJV

Let us therefore come boldly to the throne of grace, that we may obtain mercy and find grace to help in time of need.

HEBREWS 4:16 NKJV

Strength is born in the deep silence of long-suffering hearts, not amid joy.

—FELICIA HEMANS

When pain is to be borne, a little courage helps more than much knowledge, a little human sympathy more than much courage, and the least tincture of the love of God more than all.

—C. S. LEWIS

Romantic Love

Box of Chocolates

Love is very patient and kind, never jealous or envious, never boastful or proud, never haughty or selfish or rude. Love does not demand its own way. It is not irritable or touchy. It does not hold grudges and will hardly even notice when others do it wrong. It is never glad about injustice, but rejoices whenever truth wins out.

—1 Corinthians 13:4–6 TLB

In movies, music, television, and just about any other mainstream media, love is spelled s-e-x. There's no denying that sexual attraction is indeed one aspect of romantic love. According to God's Word, however, sex is reserved for marriage—a detail often overlooked by Hollywood. But that's not the only thing today's media culture overlooks. True love is far richer and far more complex than a slow motion, gauzy-lensed romp in the hay.

Take a look at 1 Corinthians 13—the familiar love chapter of the Bible. In this passage, you can learn a great deal about what true love ought to look like. Consider some of these qualities described by Paul:

Love is patient. When you love someone, you need to learn a new walking pace—both figuratively and literally—one that matches that of your love interest. Perhaps you're the kind of person who moves from point A to point B as quickly as possible and without a sideways glance. What will you do if your partner prefers to window-shop along the way? Learn the rhythms and patterns of the person you love. Also, allow your partner to move along in the relationship at his or her own pace. Don't rush commitment—that may take time.

Love is kind. Though the early romance period in a relationship is often defined by kind acts, that kindness ought to stretch on into the later period of the relationship as well. Delivering flowers, sharing words of encouragement, offering a helping hand—each of these is just as important for a long-married couple as for a newly dating couple. Kind acts build depth into love and are long remembered.

Love is never jealous. Now that's a tough one. Jealousy is a tricky tiger to tame. But it's easier than you think. The way you battle jealousy is with trust. The more you learn to trust your partner, the less jealousy you'll experience. Trust is obviously built over time, so be patient with this one in yourself and in your partner.

Love is never selfish. This is another difficult one. Early in a relationship, it may seem easy to act unselfishly. Ironically, that is in part because of a selfish motive—to gain the love of the person you care about. But true unselfish love is all about considering the feelings and needs of the other person above your own. It's not about what you can get from the relationship; rather, it is about what you can give to it. Granted, as a fallible human, you'll probably never fully escape the this-is-what-I-want mode of thinking, but that must be tempered if you are to grow in love together.

Love doesn't demand its own way. "I always watch football!" "I always go for a walk on Sunday afternoon!" When you and your partner discover differences—and you will—look first for a way to serve the interest of the other person. Be honest about what you believe or want to do, but look for a way to serve your partner. Seek balance in your relationship by serving one another's interests and learning to compromise.

Love is not irritable or touchy. True, but there are indeed times when you may be less-than-pleasant to be around. In the context of a romantic relationship, this caution might read: Love knows when it's time to get or give a little space. Learn to support your partner when things aren't going well, and also when your partner needs a little time alone.

Love doesn't hold grudges. In any romantic relationship, there are bound to be disagreements. There will also be plenty of mistakes made by both parties. Practice forgiveness whenever necessary in your romantic relationship. A grudge serves only to distance partners from one another. If the grievance is serious, consider talking with a counselor together. The longer a grudge is held, the closer a couple moves toward acceptance of the idea they shouldn't be together.

Love that is rooted in these qualities is the kind of love God intended for couples. Practice these in your romantic relationship and you will discover a depth to love that far exceeds that portrayed on the silver screen.

May all who search for you be filled with joy and gladness.
Psalm 40:16 NLT

I Will

Know that the world's view of romantic love is distorted.   *yes* _____   *no* _____

Explore what it meant to be patient in a love relationship.   *yes* _____   *no* _____

Practice kindness often in my relationships.   *yes* _____   *no* _____

Avoid jealousy by growing trust with my partner.   *yes* _____   *no* _____

Seek to serve my partner's needs and wants above my own.   *yes* _____   *no* _____

Learn when I need to give my partner space or when I need my own space.   *yes* _____   *no* _____

Things to Do

☐ *If you're in a romantic relationship, read 1 Corinthians 13 together with your partner. Talk about what it means to you.*

☐ *Write your own version of 1 Corinthians 13 using language that matches your current love life situation.*

☐ *Watch classic romance movies and look for evidence of the aspects of love Paul described in 1 Corinthians 13.*

☐ *Interview couples randomly, asking the question: "What does love mean to you?"*

☐ *Study the relationship between Jacob and Rachel in Genesis 29 and draw a conclusion about the love they shared.*

☐ *Look up the word love in a dictionary.*

Things to Remember

Set me as a seal upon your heart, as a seal upon your arm; for love is as strong as death, jealousy as cruel as the grave; its flames are flames of fire, a most vehement flame.

SONG OF SOLOMON 8:6 NKJV

Do as God does. After all, you are his dear children. Let love be your guide. Christ loved us and offered his life for us as a sacrifice that pleases God.

EPHESIANS 5:1–2 CEV

Let love be without hypocrisy. Abhor what is evil. Cling to what is good.
—Romans 12:9 NKJV

Jacob kissed Rachel and cried.

GENESIS 29:11 NCV

Love never gives up, never loses faith, is always hopeful, and endures through every circumstance.

1 CORINTHIANS 13:7 NKJV

Jesus said, "A new commandment I give to you, that you love one another; as I have loved you, that you also love one another."

JOHN 13:34 NKJV

Comfort each other and edify one
another, just as you also are doing.

1 THESSALONIANS 5:11 NKJV

Above all things have fervent love for
one another, for "love will cover a
multitude of sins."

1 PETER 4:8 NKJV

This is love, that we walk according to
His commandments. This is the
commandment, that as you have heard
from the beginning, you should walk in
it.

2 JOHN 5:6 NKJV

Jacob served seven years for Rachel, and
they seemed only a few days to him
because of the love he had for her.

GENESIS 29:20 NKJV

Many waters cannot quench love, nor
can the floods drown it.

SONG OF SOLOMON 8:7 NKJV

Unfailing love surrounds those who
trust the LORD.

PSALM 32:10 NLT

Love does not
consist in gazing at
each other but in
looking outward
together in the
same direction.

—ANTOINE DE SAINT-
EXUPÉRY

Love seeks one
thing only: the
good of the one
loved. It leaves all
the other secondary
effects to take care
of themselves.
Love, therefore, is
its own reward.

—THOMAS MERTON

Loving Your Neighbors

Samaritan I Am

Jesus said to him, "'You shall love the LORD your God with all your heart, with all your soul, and with all your mind.' This is the first and greatest commandment. And the second is like it: 'You shall love your neighbor as yourself.'"

—Matthew 22:37–39 NKJV

When a Pharisee asked Jesus which was the greatest commandment, he intended to trap Jesus, certain that by singling out one commandment, Jesus couldn't fairly represent the rest of them. However, Jesus' answer bypassed the trap as summed up all the commandments in just two: love God with all your heart, mind, and soul; and love your neighbor as yourself. This first commandment is at the very core of faith. But Jesus didn't stop there. By saying the second commandment is "like the first," Jesus plainly highlighted the importance of loving your neighbor. Elsewhere in the Bible, Jesus described loving your neighbor as reaching out to someone in need (see the story of the Good Samaritan in Luke 10:25–37).

Loving your neighbors begins with knowing who your neighbors are. And who are they? Anyone you come in contact with while you go through your day—including people you don't know and people you don't normally get along with.

Next, loving your neighbors asks that you open your eyes and heart to their needs. Be intentional about uncovering your neighbors' needs.

The Samaritan in Jesus' story chose to help the man who was lying by the side of the road, even though he didn't know the whole story of the man's predicament. A nonjudgmental attitude is an important component in loving your neighbors. You need to know, however, that you can't help everyone who has a need. It's simply not physically or emotionally possible. Ask for God's wisdom on this as you encounter opportunities to show love.

For those people you know well (they're your neighbors too), you can show love by anticipating needs. A spouse who is working long hours on the job would undoubtedly feel loved if you cooked dinner or offered to take him or her out to a restaurant at the end of the day. A friend whose car is in the shop would feel loved if you offered to be his or her taxi for the week. Sometimes practical, simple actions are the best ways to show love.

You can also love your neighbors by simply telling them you care. Use the phone or e-mail. Send a note. Tell the person you were just thinking about him or her and wanted to say "I care." Whenever you go out of your way to say "You're important to me," you express love for others in a significant and memorable way.

I Will

Know that "love your neighbor" is the second
greatest commandment.

yes   *no*

Understand that loving my neighbors sometimes
means helping to meet their needs.

yes   *no*

Recognize that "neighbor" could include anyone I
might encounter in life.

yes   *no*

Attempt to keep my eyes and heart open to the
needs of others.

yes   *no*

Avoid the trap of judging whether or not someone is
worthy of my love.

yes   *no*

Show love to people I know well by anticipating
needs.

yes   *no*

Things to Do

☐ *Ask God to prepare your heart for opportunities to love others.*

☐ *Write the story of the Good Samaritan using a modern scenario.*

☐ *Come up with one creative way to show love to someone you know well
and do it before the end of the day.*

☐ *Watch a favorite video together with a friend.*

☐ *Write a note telling a friend or family member you care about them,
then mail or deliver that note.*

☐ *Make a list of the ways you've loved your neighbors in the past week.*

Things to Remember

Whoever compels you to go one mile, go with him two.

MATTHEW 5:41 NKJV

Jesus said, "Whoever gives one of these little ones only a cup of cold water in the name of a disciple, assuredly, I say to you, he shall by no means lose his reward."

MATTHEW 10:42 NKJV

Beloved, let us love one another, for love is of God; and everyone who loves is born of God and knows God.

1 JOHN 4:7 NKJV

I try to please everyone in everything I do. I don't just do what I like or what is best for me, but what is best for them so they may be saved.

1 CORINTHIANS 10:33 NKJV

Warn those who are lazy, comfort those who are frightened, take tender care of those who are weak, and be patient with everyone.

1 THESSALONIANS 5:14 TLB

Welcome people into your home and don't grumble about it.

1 PETER 4:9 CEV

The love of our neighbor is the only door out of the dungeon of self.

—GEORGE MACDONALD

The good neighbor looks beyond the external accidents and discerns those inner qualities that make all men human and, therefore, brothers.

—MARTIN LUTHER KING JR.

Rest

A Day for You

On the seventh day God ended His work which He had done, and He rested on the seventh day from all His work which He had done.

—Genesis 2:2 NKJV

If *busy* describes your life, you're a member of a growing club. As the pace of the world picks up (faster travel, faster Internet access, faster computers, faster food), busy-ness becomes the norm rather than the exception in life.

When God set the world into motion, he also set a pattern that has become a model for the typical week. God created the world in six days, and on the seventh day He rested. God made a pretty important statement by taking one day off. The God of the universe didn't need to rest. But He chose to, and it was recorded in Scripture so all who would read God's Word would know the value He placed on taking time to rest.

Whether you're an executive in a high-pressure job or a stay-at-home parent in a high-pressure home, you know the toll a busy day can take. Rest is just about the only way to keep the temper from flaring and the mistakes from mounting. It gives you time to reflect on the past week and look forward to the next. And it gives you space to allow God to speak to you.

Here are a few ideas for resting. First, select a day you can dedicate to rest. Lots of people choose Sunday for their rest day.

Look for a way to minimize distractions on your rest day. Keep the TV off. Don't schedule any appointments. Do your best to limit the number of visitors to your home. If you relax best by puttering around a garden or by uncluttering a room—go ahead and do this. Just be sure to select activities that give you time to reflect and time to imagine possibilities.

Invite other members of the household to participate in the rest day too, if schedules allow. When everyone buys into the idea of a day of rest, it's a whole lot easier for you to really get the rest you need. You may want to consider going to a neutral site for part of your rest day—a park or a quiet coffeehouse, for example. This is especially important if other members of your household aren't observing the same rest day as you.

The most important thing to do when you're resting is to relax. Take deep breaths and enjoy God's air. Breathe in the sights and sounds of nature, and, most important, breathe in God's Spirit. Let yourself ease into a time of silent communion.

I Will

Understand that God created the model for taking time to rest.   *yes*   *no*

Accept that my life can sometimes become too busy.   *yes*   *no*

Recognize that rest is important.   *yes*   *no*

Look for ways to rest so I can reflect on the past and look forward to the future.   *yes*   *no*

Choose a day to be my rest day.   *yes*   *no*

Minimize distractions on my rest day.   *yes*   *no*

Breathe in God's Spirit during my day of rest and be restored.   *yes*   *no*

Things to Do

☐ *Choose one day that will be your rest day. Mark this on your calendar.*

☐ *Make a list of things to avoid on your rest day. Post this near your calendar.*

☐ *Look up the word rest in a concordance and read the related Scripture passages.*

☐ *Talk with family members or friends about what a day of rest ought to look like. Make a plan to use some of these ideas.*

☐ *Gather a number of soothing CDs from your collection (instrumental may be best) and put them in a special location so you can easily access them on your rest day.*

Things to Remember

Abraham said, "Please let a little water be brought, and wash your feet, and rest yourselves under the tree."

GENESIS 18:4 NKJV

I said, "Oh, that I had wings like a dove! I would fly away and be at rest.

PSALM 55:6 NKJV

Jesus said, "Take my yoke upon you. Let me teach you, because I am humble and gentle, and you will find rest for your souls."

MATTHEW 11:29 NLT

[Jesus and the disciples] departed to a deserted place in the boat by themselves.

MARK 6:32 NKJV

Since God has left us the promise that we may enter his rest, let us be very careful so none of you will fail to enter.

HEBREWS 4:1 NCV

The LORD said, "Six days you shall do your work, and on the seventh day you shall rest, that your ox and your donkey may rest, and the son of your female servant and the stranger may be refreshed."

EXODUS 23:12 NKJV

All the troubles of life come upon us because we refuse to sit quietly for a while each day in our rooms.

—BLAISE PASCAL

God is a tranquil Being, and abides in a tranquil eternity. So must thy spirit become a tranquil and clear little pool, wherein the serene light of God can be mirrored.

—GERHARD TERSTEEGEN

Infusion

My health fails; my spirits droop, yet God remains! He is the strength of my heart; he is mine forever!

—Psalm 73:26 TLB

One thing is certain: People are hungry for more physical energy or strength in their lives. What many are really in search of is spiritual strength—the kind of strength that can help them endure physically, mentally, and emotionally.

The psalmist drew a familiar illustration with his depiction of failing health and drooping spirits in Psalm 73:26—he could just as well have been describing a typical day in your life or the life of a friend. But he didn't write this psalm to complain. Instead, he wrote it to point to the answer for diminished energy—God.

God's storehouse of strength is dependable and bottomless. He can provide for physical, mental, and emotional needs—all through the spiritual conduit. According to the psalmist, God's strength is available no matter what circumstances you're going through. There is a source of energy far beyond what you might need and as close as a prayer.

Exercise gurus will tell you that the more you exercise, the greater your energy level. This is true also for spiritual matters. Of course, if you haven't exercised in a while, there is a bit of pain to endure while you ramp up to a healthy regimen. Through daily Bible reading, regular Bible study, frequent prayer, and other spiritual endeavors, you'll develop stronger spiritual muscles that will give you more energy than ever.

Another way you can gain strength is to look at how God has shown up in history. For example, just when the Israelites thought they could endure no longer as slaves, God brought Moses to a position of power and provided a hope that freedom was around the corner. And just in time, God opened the waters of the Red Sea and provided a safe passage for the Israelites. Seeing that God has provided in the past can give you hope that He will be there for you too.

You can also gain strength from close friends and family members. God created the idea of community and the institution of family in part to give each person a support system for the difficult times of life. Their encouragement, prayers, and wisdom can help you regain the strength you need to move forward.

You can count on the fact that you'll be emotionally, physically, or mentally drained at times. But you can also count on the fact that you have a renewable source of energy. Plug into God and God's will, and you will be recharged.

I Will

Accept that I could use more energy at times.   yes   no

Know that the best source for spiritual energy is
God.   yes   no

Be reassured that God's storehouse of strength
won't run out.   yes   no

Exercise my spiritual life through Bible reading,
Bible study, and prayer.   yes   no

Reflect on ways God has shown up in the past and
count on God's consistency in responding to a cry
for strength.   yes   no

Consider seeking strength from close friends and
family members.   yes   no

Things to Do

☐ Choose a partner (family member or friend) and ask this person to be
your spiritual exercise partner for a month. Plan on meeting together
regularly to explore God's Word.

☐ Study how God has acted in history by reading the story of the
Israelite's quest for relief and renewed strength in Exodus 1—15.

☐ Go to a gym and work out or take a long walk if you are able to.
Compare these kinds of physical exercise to spiritual exercise.

☐ Talk with a close friend or family member about what it means to be a
support person in times when your strength is diminished.

☐ Make a list of three or more ways you can regain physical, mental, and
emotional strength.

Things to Remember

In the day when I cried out, You answered me, and made me bold with strength in my soul.

PSALM 138:3 NKJV

The glory of the young is their strength; the gray hair of experience is the splendor of the old.

PROVERBS 20:29 NLT

Do not fear, for I am with you; do not be dismayed, for I am your God. I will strengthen you and help you; I will uphold you with my righteous right hand.

ISAIAH 41:10 NIV

Wisdom strengthens the wise more than ten rulers of the city.

ECCLESIASTES 7:19 NKJV

Paul wrote: I take pleasure in infirmities, in reproaches, in needs, in persecutions, in distresses, for Christ's sake. For when I am weak, then I am strong.

2 CORINTHIANS 12:10 NKJV

Jesus said, "I am sending upon you what my Father promised; so stay here in the city until you have been clothed with power from on high."

LUKE 24:49 NRSV

When You are our strength, it is strength indeed, but when our strength is our own it is only weakness.

—SAINT AUGUSTINE OF HIPPO

When we feel us too bold, remember our own feebleness. When we feel us too faint, remember Christ's strength.

—SIR THOMAS MORE

Standing Up for Your Beliefs

Confident Conversation

Paul wrote: I am not ashamed of the gospel of Christ, for it is the power of God to salvation for everyone who believes, for the Jew first and also for the Greek.

—*Romans 1:16 NKJV*

In a society that's founded on the ideals of free speech, free assembly, and freedom of religious choice, who would think that standing up for your beliefs would even be an issue? It is precisely because there are so many different beliefs that you need to know how to stand tall in what you believe. In subtle and not-so-subtle ways, coworkers, friends, neighbors, family members, and the media may challenge your belief.

Today, the chances that you'll be martyred for your beliefs are slim. But that doesn't mean you won't be put into situations where your faith is challenged. How should you respond? How can you stand up for your beliefs?

The apostle Paul got his strength from God's Spirit. By the power of the Spirit, Paul spoke with conviction about his beliefs. Paul probably wasn't a big man physically, but his words loomed large because of his inner strength.

Know what you believe. It's difficult to stand up for

what you believe if you don't know what that is. Go to the Bible, talk with Christian friends or church leaders, and come to conclusions about the nonnegotiable aspects of your faith. Know why you believe what you do.

Know when to speak out. There will be times when it's inappropriate to share what you believe. There will also be times when the occasion arises for you to tell others what is important to you. Don't miss out on opportunities to speak up in defense of your faith.

Understand that there's a risk involved in standing up for what you believe. You'll need to weigh the risks. Is it a good idea to get into a potentially charged discussion with a supervisor over issues of faith? Is it worth the risk to confront a friend who is making terrible life decisions that could harm others? Ask God for wisdom to know what is right.

When you do stand up for your beliefs, you may discover you're not alone. Others who may have less strength of conviction, but similar beliefs, may gain strength from your resolve.

When you speak with conviction, people listen. Some people may disagree with your words, but most will be drawn to your confidence. Be prepared when you stand up for your beliefs to follow up with those who are intrigued by what you have to say.

Know that God smiles on you when you don't shy away from your beliefs. Stand tall and know that God is beside you.

I Will

Look to God's Spirit for inner strength.   *yes*   *no*

Know what I believe.   *yes*   *no*

Know that my faith may be challenged.   *yes*   *no*

Understand that it's important to be confident in
my beliefs.   *yes*   *no*

Recognize that there is risk involved in standing up
for my beliefs.   *yes*   *no*

Be prepared to follow up with those who are
intrigued by my beliefs.   *yes*   *no*

Gain confidence from the fact that God stands
beside me when I stand up for my faith.   *yes*   *no*

Things to Do

☐ *Ask God for confidence and wisdom to live out your faith confidently and without apology.*

☐ *Write down your personal beliefs and note those that are nonnegotiable.*

☐ *Read the book of Romans and see what you can learn from Paul's confidence that can help to build your own resolve.*

☐ *Invite a group of Christian friends to discuss the challenges and joys of standing up for beliefs.*

☐ *Read Foxe's Book of Martyrs, or Jesus Freaks by dc Talk and The Voice of the Martyrs, and consider how you might have responded to the situations faced by each martyr.*

Things to Remember

This is His commandment: that we should believe on the name of His Son Jesus Christ and love one another, as He gave us commandment.

1 JOHN 3:23 NKJV

Paul dwelt two whole years in his own rented house, and received all who came to him, preaching the kingdom of God and teaching the things which concern the Lord Jesus Christ with all confidence, no one forbidding him.

ACTS 28:30–31 NKJV

We make it our aim, whether present or absent, to be well pleasing to Him.

2 CORINTHIANS 5:7 NKJV

He commanded us to preach to the people, and to testify that it is He who was ordained by God to be Judge of the living and the dead.

ACTS 10:42 NKJV

I will always sing about the LORD's love; I will tell of his loyalty from now on.

PSALM 89:1 NCV

I will declare Your name to My brethren; in the midst of the assembly I will praise You.

PSALM 22:22 NKJV

You never know how much you really believe anything until its truth or falsehood becomes a matter of life and death to you.

—C. S. LEWIS

Never, for sake of peace and quiet, deny your own experience or convictions.

—DAG HAMMARSKJOLD

Honesty

Such a Lonely Word

Dishonest scales are an abomination to the LORD, but a just weight is His delight.

—Proverbs 11:1 NKJV

A heated exchange between two characters in a popular movie went something like this: "You want the truth?" "Yes, I want the truth." "You can't handle the truth!"

While this makes for a powerful dramatic moment in the film, it also expresses a sad truth about the way people view the truth, as if it is an option. Why else would people use the phrase "Well, to be perfectly honest" if they weren't usually perfectly honest? In a world forged by deception (keep in mind Satan's role in Eden, Genesis 3), complete honesty is rare. But whether the truth is bent through a little white lie or twisted through blatant fraud, God's response is the same: A lie is a lie is a lie.

Proverbs 11:1 uses the analogy of a dishonest scale to depict the loathsomeness of lying. In a culture defined by tall tales, that's a tall order. But it is possible.

Begin by accepting that honesty is God's way. God

didn't hide the dangers that Adam and Eve would face if they ate the fruit of the tree of life. He didn't sugarcoat the result of disobeying God. Throughout biblical history, God has spoken directly and honestly with His people. He wants you to do the same.

Admit your mistakes and bad choices. You may need to ask for forgiveness from someone you've lied to. Choose an appropriate time and place, ask God to give you the words to speak, and take care of that situation. You have to deal with the lies that you may now be living before you can become an honest person.

Honesty isn't the same thing as saying whatever happens to be on your mind without regard for the feelings of others. When you speak the truth, do so in love. It's not always easy for someone to hear the truth, but that doesn't make it any less important. Choose your words wisely—after seeking God's direction—and wrap them in concern for the other person before you speak. There will be times when a person is hurt by the words you share, but when the truth is spoken in love, that pain is only temporary.

Honesty is a risky business. It's tempting to defer or deflect the truth because of the fear of rejection or pain. Speak the truth anyway. The rewards for truthfulness far outweigh the risks of dishonesty. Which would you prefer, God's delight or His displeasure?

I Will

Ponder the fact that many people see telling the truth as an option.   *yes*   *no*

Know that God despises dishonesty.   *yes*   *no*

Accept that honesty is God's way.   *yes*   *no*

Admit my mistakes and ask for forgiveness from those I've lied to.   *yes*   *no*

Be considerate of others' feelings when I speak the truth.   *yes*   *no*

Know that the rewards of honesty outweigh the risks.   *yes*   *no*

Seek to delight God by living honestly.   *yes*   *no*

Things to Do

☐ Ask God to give you the courage to be honest in all areas of life.

☐ Read the two quotes in this meditation and then write one of your own about honesty.

☐ List the most recent lie you've told someone. Then, if appropriate, contact that person and ask for forgiveness for your lie.

☐ Interview five or six people at random asking the question, "Is it ever okay to lie? Why or why not?"

☐ Make a list of areas in your life where you need to be more truthful.

☐ Talk with a friend about the challenge in speaking the truth to someone when that truth could hurt.

Things to Remember

We cannot do anything against the truth, but only for the truth.

2 CORINTHIANS 13:8 NCV

LORD, who may abide in Your tabernacle? Who may dwell in Your holy hill? He who walks uprightly, and works righteousness, and speaks the truth in his heart.

PSALM 15:1 NKJV

An honest man's the noblest work of God.

—ALEXANDER POPE

Moreover they did not require an account from the men into whose hand they delivered the money to be paid to workmen, for they dealt faithfully.

2 KINGS 12:15 NKJV

Honesty is the first chapter of the book of wisdom.

—THOMAS JEFFERSON

Jesus said, "You know the commandments: 'Do not commit adultery,' 'Do not murder,' 'Do not steal,' 'Do not bear false witness,' 'Do not defraud,' 'Honor your father and your mother.'"

MARK 10:19 NKJV

The king rejoices when his people are truthful and fair.

PROVERBS 16:13 TLB

Use honest weights and measures, so that you will enjoy a long life in the land the Lord your God is giving you.

DEUTERONOMY 25:15 NKJV

Other Books in the Checklist for Life Series

Available at your local bookstore October 2002:

Checklist for Life for Women
ISBN 0-7852-6462-0

Checklist for Life for Men
ISBN 0-7852-6463-9

Checklist for Life for Teens
ISBN 0-7852-6461-2